DayOne

Thoughts Fixed & Affections Flaming

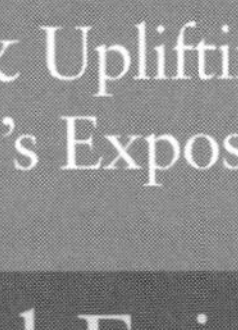

Pithy, Interesting & Uplifting Comments from Matthew Henry's Exposition of the Bible

Nigel Faithfull

Matthew Henry's commentary is like a mine loaded with diamonds. Nigel Faithfull gathers these diamonds by the handful and brings them sparkling into the light.
—Joel R. Beeke, Puritan Reformed Theological Seminary

First printed 2012

ISBN 978–1–84625–309–6

Unless otherwise indicated, Scripture quotations in this publication are from the **King James (Authorized) Version** (**KJV**), Crown copyright

British Library Cataloguing in Publication Data available

Published by Day One Publications
Ryelands Road, Leominster, HR6 8NZ
☎ 01568 613 740 FAX 01568 611 473
email—sales@dayone.co.uk
web site—www.dayone.co.uk
North America—email—usasales@dayone.co.uk

Cover design by Wayne McMaster
Printed by TJ International Ltd

Matthew Henry's massive commentary on the whole Bible is like a mine loaded with diamonds. Nigel Faithfull gathers these diamonds by the handful and brings them sparkling into the light. This is a versatile resource. You can use its index to look up Henry's wisdom on a particular topic or you can use it along with your daily reading through the Bible. Either way it is bound to bless. May God make the 350th anniversary of Henry's birth into an occasion for many to discover anew the glory of Christ shining in the writings of Matthew Henry and his fellow Puritans.

Professor Joel R. Beeke, President, Puritan Reformed Theological Seminary, Grand Rapids, MI, USA

Dr Nigel Faithfull was a member of our congregation in Aberystwyth for forty years. He sat at my feet, grave, thoughtful and encouraging. He often had helpful words to share with me in response to the preaching. He read much, widely and well, the best books. As a scientist he was especially interested in the biblical doctrine of creation. Now it is my time to sit at his feet and learn from what he has gleaned from the greatest of Puritan commentators, Matthew Henry. It would be an achievement to read through his commentary on the entire Bible. Dr Faithfull has done more than that; he has gathered together aphorisms and insights from the writer and also indexed them. What we have is a wonderful overview of the Christian faith to ponder and reflect on. I have found the contents stimulating and inspiring. This is truly a store of priceless treasure, such choice statements of profound truth. It affords rich instruction and help to all Christians.

Dr Geoff Thomas, Pastor of Alfred Place Baptist Church in Aberystwyth, Wales

Courtesy of the Trustees of the Congregational Library, London

To my dear grandchildren,

Tristan, James, Ffion and Nathan

Contents

Acknowledgements

I would never have embarked on this enterprise if I had not been given the nine-volume set of Matthew Henry's *Exposition of the Old and New Testaments* as a young man back in 1965. This set had been rescued by my godly father when clearing out the books of his late father, and he presented it to me, who, at that time, had never before heard of it. A friend, Richard Russell, informed me that Spurgeon had said that one should sell one's last shirt to purchase it, so it accompanied me to university at Aberystwyth. I am therefore grateful to my late father for giving it, my friend for recommending it, and the Lord for his providence.

I thank Dr Gwyn Davies of Aberystwyth for reminding me to mention Matthew Henry's Welsh roots, and Dr David Wykes, Director of Dr Williams's Library, London, for providing a reference to his research essay on the persecution of Matthew Henry and his congregation. I am grateful to Jim Holmes of Day One for directing and marketing the publication, and to Suzanne Mitchell for her editorial skills.

I am also indebted to Dr Geoff Thomas (Aberystwyth) and Dr Joel Beeke (Grand Rapids, MI) for their generous endorsements, and particularly for Geoff's ministry during the forty-five years my family and I lived in Aberystwyth, when we rejoiced in those same grand doctrines of the faith written about in Henry's exposition.

Finally, I thank my wife, Eileen, who has shown much patience while I have been glued to the computer monitor, and provides the support of one sharing the same doctrines to be found within the covers of this book.

Nigel T. Faithfull
April 2012

Matthew Henry (18 October 1662—22 June 1714), the renowned expositor of the Bible, had a unique style, and his famous commentary included many pithy phrases, apophthegms, aphorisms, interesting observations and wise, proverb-like sayings. For example, he coined the expression 'creature-comforts'. In his commentary, many memorable phrases are preceded by 'Note, …', or 'Observe …' George Whitefield noted such a saying in his journal in 1738: 'Had this sentence out of Henry much pressed upon my heart to comfort me in my retirement. "The mower loses no time whilst he is whetting his scythe."'[1] Two years earlier, Whitefield, having returned from ministering in London to his small congregation at Oxford, recorded, 'Oh what a delightful life did I lead there! What communion did I daily enjoy with God! How sweetly did my hours in private glide away in reading and praying over Mr Henry's *Comment upon the Scriptures*.'[2]

Robert Hall, George Whitefield and Charles Spurgeon all used and heartily commended the work, with Whitefield reading it through four times—the last time on his knees.[3] Spurgeon stated, 'Every minister ought to read Matthew Henry entirely and carefully through once at least.'[4] The Baptist preacher and educator John Ryland Sr. (1723–1792) testified, 'It is impossible for a person of piety and taste to read the Exposition of Mr Henry without wishing to be shut out from all the world to read it through without one moment's interruption.'[5]

The year 2010 marked the 300th anniversary of the publication of Henry's other noted work, *A Method for Prayer*, recently republished as *A Way to Pray*;[6] 2012 marks the 350th anniversary of Henry's birth. The following compilation has been gleaned over a period of forty years from Henry's nine-volume exposition, of almost 7.6 million words, which was published by James Nisbet in 1866. This may go some way to satisfy Warren Wiersbe's hope that 'Perhaps some enterprising reader could mine some of Matthew Henry's pithy sayings and put them into a book for us'.[7]

Notes

1 *George Whitefield's Journals* (2nd. edn.; London: Banner of Truth, 1965), p. 169.
2 Ibid., p. 78.
3 'Matthew Henry (1662–1714)', at www.tlogical.net/biohenry.htm; accessed March 2012.
4 **Charles H. Spurgeon,** *Commenting and Commentaries: Lectures Addressed to the Students of The Pastor's College, Metropolitan Tabernacle* (New York: Sheldon & Co., 1876), p. 14; available at archive.org/stream/commentingandco00spurgoog#page/n6/mode/2up; accessed April 2012.
5 Quoted at 'Matthew Henry 1662–1714, English Minister and Bible Commentator', at www.eaec.org/faithhallfame/matthewhenry.htm; accessed March 2012.
6 **Matthew Henry,** *A Way to Pray* (Edinburgh: Banner of Truth, 2010).
7 **Warren W. Wiersbe,** *50 People Every Christian Should Know* (Grand Rapids, MI: Baker, 2009), p. 29.

Biography of Matthew Henry

His family background: royal connections

In order to understand the life and comments of Matthew Henry, it is helpful to look into his ancestry and background.[1] His grandfather was John Henry (1590–1652), the son of Henry Williams of Briton Ferry, between Swansea and Neath in South Wales; he took his father's Christian name as his surname, in line with an old Welsh custom. John Henry became a courtier under James I (who reigned in England from 1603–1625) and then Charles I (who reigned 1625–1649). His son (Matthew's father) Philip (1631–1696) had as godparents the Earls of Pembroke and Carlisle, and the Countess of Salisbury. As a child, Philip used to play at St James's Palace with the somewhat younger Princes Charles and James, later to become Charles II and James II. It is no surprise that Philip's early lifestyle was also that of a courtier and that he retained his royalist allegiance. The Civil War broke out when he was eleven years old and lasted on and off for the next nine years. Philip favoured the restoration of the monarchy with the return of his friend as Charles II, who reigned from 1660–1685.

PHILIP HENRY: SCHOLAR AND CHRISTIAN

At the age of twelve Philip attended Westminster School, becoming proficient in Greek and Latin. His mother took him to hear the preaching of the Westminster Divines, including Stephen Marshal (1594/5–1655), under whom he was 'begotten again unto a lively hope',[2] and Thomas Case (1598–1682). He was also moved by the ministry of William Bridge of Great Yarmouth and, later, Norwich, the author of *A Lifting Up for the Downcast*.

In 1647, aged sixteen, he entered Christ Church, Oxford, graduating with a BA in 1651, the year Cromwell appointed John Owen as Dean of Christ Church. He proceeded to an MA in 1652. Owen's recommendation helped Philip become a tutor for Judge John Puleston's sons, and Puleston later appointed him to Worthenbury Chapel, Iscoyd (now Bangor Is-y-coed), in 1654. Following Philip's induction in 1657 at Prees in Shropshire, Puleston formally gave him the living in 1659 and built him a new parsonage.

NONCONFORMITY

Philip Henry's views on church government were against the prelacy, or episcopacy (that is, government by bishops), and for the Presbyterian system that had ordained himself and John Owen (that is, government by presbyters under a moderator). As for the Independents, Philip, in his diary, commended them for their church discipline, love and their correspondence with one another. Although favouring the parish system, he had scruples about using the newly issued *Book of Common Prayer* (1662). He attended Anglican Communion services, but refused to kneel at the altar rail, as this was contrary to the notion of a supper and more in keeping with the idolatrous practices of Catholics.

Although Charles II was tolerant of differing modes of worship, his government was not, and trying times lay ahead, particularly with the publishing of the Corporation Act (1661), which prevented Nonconformists from taking public office, and the Act of Uniformity (1662), under which over 2,000 clergymen were expelled from their churches in the Great Ejection of 1662 because they refused to take the oath not 'to endeavour any change or alteration of government either in Church or State', and to declare their 'unfeigned assent to all and everything contained in and prescribed in ... The Book of Common Prayer',[3] which also included the episcopal ordination of ministers. Philip Henry was one of the ejected ministers and so left Worthenbury to take residence at the estate of his wife, Katherine (1629–1707), at Broad Oak and Bronington, Flintshire. Their son John (1661–1667) was born at Worthenbury, but Matthew and his four sisters were born at Broad Oak. Matthew was baptized at Whitewell, but Philip refused to assist, because he would not make the sign of the cross.

Hot on the heels of the above-mentioned Acts came the Conventicle Act (1664), which outlawed the meeting together for worship of more than five non-family members, and the Five Mile Act, which prevented ejected ministers from living within five miles of their previous parishes and from teaching in schools. The king, aware of the harshness of these Acts (known as the Clarendon Code), issued a Declaration of Indulgence in 1672. Philip now exercised his preaching ministry from Broad Oak. This short interval of peace came to an end when Parliament forced the king to withdraw the Declaration in 1679.

Charles II died on 6 February 1685, and on 11 June the exiled Duke of Monmouth, his illegitimate son, landed at Lyme Regis in Dorset with a small force in an attempt to topple the new Catholic king, James II. At this time the authorities were very suspicious of meetings and possible plots, and Philip was arrested for defying the Conventicle Act and incarcerated in Chester Castle for three weeks.

By 1687, conditions for Nonconformists had improved somewhat, and Matthew Henry, who was now aged twenty-four, was able to be ordained at Broad Oak on 9 May by his father and five other colleagues. During the following year, all five of Matthew's siblings were married at Whitewell Chapel. Then in 1689 the Act of Toleration was passed; this allowed Nonconformists their own places of worship and their own teachers, if they accepted certain oaths of allegiance. Philip died on 24 June 1696 and was buried at Whitchurch. Each of his four daughters was bequeathed a copy of Matthew Poole's *Annotations*, while the rest of Philip's library went to his wife and Matthew. Matthew preached one of his father's funeral sermons.

Matthew Henry

In order to complete the summary of the life of Philip Henry, we have jumped ahead in the life of his son. Matthew Henry was born prematurely on 18 October 1662 at Broad Oak, Flintshire. He was a sickly child, but he was intended for the ministry from an early age. He was educated at home, becoming proficient in the learned languages, with a particular aptitude for Hebrew. There is credible evidence that he could read portions of the Scriptures when he was only three years old. According to his own reckoning, his conversion took place before he turned eleven. It was one of his father's sermons that, in Henry's words, 'melted' him and caused him to 'inquire after Christ'.[4] His father had by this time become a well known preacher, and as early as 1658 he took a month off to visit Oxford, preaching at St Mary the Virgin, Christ Church and Corpus Christi College. He also visited London, where he preached at Westminster Abbey. Matthew would have learned from him many of his pithy sayings, together with his Nonconformist principles.

A PURITAN EDUCATION

From 1680, when Matthew was eighteen, he attended for three years the important Dissenting academy of the Puritan Thomas Doolittle at Islington. Doolittle (1630–1707) was born at Kidderminster and converted at the age of seventeen under the preaching of Richard Baxter. The Dissenters faced a period of persecution in 1683, so Doolittle had to move his academy from Islington to Battersea, and Matthew returned home before proceeding in 1685 to study law at Gray's Inn. This legal training is evident in the many forensic terms used throughout his exposition. He continued with his theological studies and attended the best preachers he could find.

ORDINATION AND MARRIAGE

Matthew was ordained privately in May 1687 by six ejected ministers and he preached his first public sermon at White-Friars, Chester, on 2 June in some converted stables. In August 1700 the growing congregation moved to a purpose-built meeting house in Crook Lane; a gallery was added in 1707. (This building was pulled down in the 1960s to build the Forum Shopping Centre.) 'We know', recorded Henry in his diary, 'how to enlarge the straitness of the place. God by his grace enlarge the straitness of our hearts.'[5] They now numbered 350 communicants, with 300 in regular attendance. Matthew married Katherine in 1687, but she died of smallpox at the age of twenty-five, leaving a daughter, also named Katherine. He married Mary five months later; together they had eight daughters and a son, Philip, who became MP for Chester.

PREACHER AND EXPOSITOR

Matthew preached in the villages around Chester and also made annual tours to Lancashire and Staffordshire. He and his congregation were abused by High Churchmen, and an attempt was made to burn down their meeting place in 1692. In a letter Matthew told his father that four pew doors, two on either side of the aisle (one being his wife's seat), had been opened and the fire kindled beneath them. As it was the middle of the night, it was a miracle the fire was discovered. 'The light and roaring of it was more terrible than one could imagine.'[6] God also overruled, in that Richard Lee, 'tho' an enemy to the Chapel', was very helpful in quenching the fire because his hay-loft adjoined it.[7]

Matthew began his *Exposition of the Old and New Testament* with comments on the Pentateuch in 1704, which was published in folio three years later; he completed the entire Old Testament in 1712. This was during the period of Queen Anne (1665–1714), daughter of James II. Although her parents were Roman Catholic, Anne was brought up as a member of the Church of England and had a Protestant governess. The Bishop of London, Henry Compton (1631/2–1713), guided her in the Christian faith and exercised an anti-Catholic bias, so she could write to her sister in 1686, when she felt herself persecuted for her faith, 'God be thanked we were not bred up in that communion, but are of a Church that is pious and sincere, and conformable in all its principles to the Scriptures.'[8] Several times in his *Exposition* Matthew gives thanks to God for this period of national peace and freedom from persecution. Thus on Esther 10:3 he comments, 'Thanks be to God, such a government as this we are blessed with, which *seeks the welfare of our people, speaking peace to all their seed.* God continue it long, very long, and grant us, under the happy protection and influence of it, to *live quiet and peaceable lives, in godliness, honesty* and charity!'

The same year he completed the Old Testament, on 18 May 1712, Matthew received a call to minister in Hackney and soon took his place among the leading ministers of his day. He published thirty other works, but only his *Exposition*, and now *A Method for Prayer*, have endured.

A METHOD FOR PRAYER

Matthew Henry referred to prayer as a 'sweet and precious duty'. He said, 'I love prayer. It is that which buckles on all the Christian's armour.'[9] Accordingly, he set about writing a manual on prayer, which he entitled *A Method for Prayer* (1710).[10] In the Preface he writes, 'When I had finished the third volume of Expositions of the Bible ... I was willing to take a little time from that work to this poor performance, in hopes it might be of some service to the generation of them that seek God.'[11] Matthew defines prayer thus: 'Prayer is the solemn and religious offering of devout acknowledgments and desires to God, or a sincere representation of holy affections, with a design to give unto God the glory due unto his name thereby, and to obtain from him promised favours, and both thro' the Mediator.'[12]

He sets out to explain the various divisions of prayer: Adoration, Confession, Petition, Thanksgiving and Intercession. Prayers for special occasions are given, but most interesting is Chapter 8, 'A Paraphrase on the Lord's Prayer, in Scripture Expressions'. He is aware that in giving examples of prayers, people might simply formally recite them, and so he comments, 'A man may write straight, without having his paper ruled.'[13]

DEATH

He had just completed his commentary on the Gospels and Acts when he died, on 22 June 1714, at the home of the Revd Joseph Mottershead, near Nantwich, as a result of a fall from his horse while on a visit to Cheshire. So much studying and lack of exercise had made him corpulent. The sorrow at his death was universal; 'there was hardly a Pulpit of the Dissenters in London but what gave Notice of the great Breach that was made upon the Church of God'.[14] He was buried on 25 June in the chancel of Holy Trinity Church, Chester, and attended by eight of the city clergy. After his death, thirteen Nonconformist ministers of varying abilities completed his New Testament exposition, referring to Matthew's notes.

His legacy

Undoubtedly, Matthew Henry's *Exposition* is a treasure bequeathed to Christ's church on earth. Spurgeon stated,

> First among the mighty [commentaries] for general usefulness we are bound to mention the man whose name is a household word, MATTHEW HENRY. He is most pious and pithy, sound and sensible, suggestive and sober, terse and trustworthy … he is deeply spiritual, heavenly, and profitable; finding good matter in every text, and from all deducing most practical and judicious lessons … It is the poor man's commentary, the old Christian's companion, suitable to everybody, instructive to all.[15]

Matthew Henry's *Exposition* was written about a hundred years after Shakespeare's plays, so the English is not as obscure as it is in those works, and one is not aware of it being too dated in modes of expression.

Baptists must make allowances for the occasions he underlines his paedobaptist views, but these are few and far between. Today, there are many more modern commentaries to choose from, but Matthew Henry's has stood the test of time. One of the most repeated quotations is on Genesis 2:21–23:

Observe: That the woman was *made of a rib out of the side of Adam*; not made out of his head to rule over him, nor out of his feet to be trampled upon by him, but out of his side to be equal with him, under his arm to be protected, and near his heart to be beloved.

There are striking notes for every occasion, such as the following examples from Genesis and Revelation. Concerning the death of a young believer he writes, 'God often takes those soonest whom he loves best, and the time they lose on earth is gained in heaven, to their unspeakable advantage. Those whose conversation in the world is truly holy shall find their removal out of it truly happy' (Gen. 5:23–24). A comment applicable to suicide or euthanasia is: 'Our lives are not so our own as that we may quit them at our own pleasure, but they are God's, and we must resign them at his pleasure; if we in any way hasten our own deaths, we are accountable to God for it' (Gen. 9:5). Concerning old age he says, 'Old age is a blessing. It is promised in the fifth commandment; it is pleasing to nature; and it affords a great opportunity for usefulness' (Gen. 15:15). Regarding prayer Henry says, 'All the saints are a praying people; none of the children of God are born dumb, a Spirit of grace is always a Spirit of adoption and supplication, teaching us to cry, *Abba, Father*' (Rev. 8:3). As for God's wrath, 'When the sins of a people reach up to heaven, the wrath of God will reach down to the earth' (Rev. 18:5). The final quote in this book exhorts us to seek the grace of Christ while we have opportunity, and points us to glory: 'Nothing should be more desired by us than that the grace of Christ may be with us in this world, to prepare us for the glory of Christ in the other world' (Rev. 22:21). There are hundreds more gems, some rather quaint but all profitable. With single-volume unabridged editions for under £30, and free online versions, this great work is now within everyone's reach.[16]

Notes

1 **J. B. Williams, (ed.),** *The Lives of Philip and Matthew Henry* (Edinburgh: Banner of Truth, 1974).

2 Ibid. The Life of Philip Henry', p. 6.

3 From 'Uniformity, Act of 19 May 1662 (England)', at www.thereformation.info/uniformityact.htm; accessed April 2012.

4 From **Matthew Henry,** 'A Catalogue of Mercies' (1675); quoted at www.sounddoctrine.net/LIBRARY/Bible%20Studies/MHenry-biography.htm; accessed April 2012.

5 **Williams,** 'The Life of Matthew Henry', in *The Lives of Philip and Matthew Henry*, p, 137, quoting from the original manuscript of Matthew Henry's Diary.

6 **David L. Wykes,** '"So Bitterly Censur'd and Revil'd": Religious Dissent and Relations with the Church of England after the Toleration Act', pp. 295–313 in **Richard Bonney and D. J. B. Trim, (eds.),** *Persecution and Pluralism: Calvinists and Religious Minorities in Early Modern Europe 1550–1700* (Bern: Peter Lang, 2006), p. 299.

7 Ibid.

8 **Edward Gregg,** 'Anne (1665–1714)', *Oxford Dictionary of National Biography* (Oxford: Oxford University Press, 2004); online edn., Jan 2012, at www.oxforddnb.com/view/article/560; accessed April 2012; citing **B. C. Brown, (ed.),** *The Letters and Diplomatic Instructions of Queen Anne* (London: Cassell, 1968), 29 April 1686, p. 16.

9 Quoted in **John Bickerton Williams,** *Memoirs of the Life, Character, and Writings of the Rev. Matthew Henry* (London: Joseph Ogle Robinson, 1829), p. 278.

10 **Matthew Henry,** *A Method for Prayer* (1710); an 1803 edition (Edinburgh: Ogle & Aikman / Leith: W. Coke) is available as a free download from books.google.co.uk.

11 Ibid., p. xi.

12 Ibid., p. iii.

13 Ibid., p. xi.

14 **William Tong,** *An Account of the Life and Death of Mr. Matthew Henry, Minister of the*

Gospel at Hackney, Who Dy'd June 22, 1714 in the 52d Year of his Age (London: W. Baynes, 1716), p. 282.

15 Charles H. Spurgeon, *Commenting and Commentaries: Lectures Addressed to the Students of The Pastor's College, Metropolitan Tabernacle* (New York: Sheldon & Co., 1876), p. 13; available at archive.org/stream/commentingandco00spurgoog#page/n6/mode/2up; accessed April 2012.

16 It is available at www.e-sword.net/downloads.html (download the e-Sword application first, then choose Matthew Henry from the 'Commentaries' available in the 'Downloads' menu); www.ccel.org/ccel/henry/mhc.i.html; handheld.softpedia.com/get/Educational/Bible/Matthew-Henrys-Commentary-on-the-Whole-Bible-MHC-CadreBible-Book-73778.shtml (Android 2.2 free version)

Topical guide to selected quotes from Matthew Henry

Topical guide to selected quotes from Matthew Henry

Ignorance Eccles. 1:17–18; 1 Tim. 1:13 (sins of ignorance)

Immanuel Matt. 1:23

Impenitence Jer. 44:27

Inheritance Josh. 18:9; 1 Sam. 15:6; Job 19:25; John 20:21 (legacy from Christ); Acts 1:4 (legacy of Spirit)

Inns Luke 10:34

Inordinate love Gen. 37:35; 48:7; 2 Sam. 24:3; Jonah 4:9

Intercession Exod. 9:29

Islanders Ezek. 27:3; Acts 13:47 (British Isles)

Jesting Zech. 12:3 (of religion)

Jewellery Ps. 73:6; Mal. 3:17 (God's jewels)

John the Baptist Matt. 3:1, 3; Luke 3:16

Joseph's coat Gen. 37:31–32; 39:18

Joy Gen. 15:12; Lev. 23:40–42; Neh. 8:10; Ps. 81:2–3; 86:4; 119:32, 162; Prov. 14:13; 29:6; Eccles. 9:7; S. of S. 5:6; Isa. 61:3; Ezek. 32:16; Joel 2:22; Nahum 3:16–17; Matt. 9:24; Luke 9:28–29; 16:22; John 8:56; 14:1; Acts 20:24

Judgment Gen. 7:12; 9:13; Exod. 5:17; 2 Chr. 26:19; Ps. 21:8; 59:13; 119:7; Prov. 18:17; Isa. 14:23; 28:11–12; 59:10; Jer. 5:31; 9:24; 27:16,22; 44:27; Ezek. 9:2; 14:9; Hosea 2:10; 4:17; 7:14 (temporal); Amos 3:15; Matt. 7:1; 18:15, 18–19 (of others); 25:20, 22; John 12:48; Rom. 14:4 (of others)

Justice Gen. 6:7; Isa. 59:4; Hosea 2:10 (God's); 5:14; John 1:25

Justification Ezek. 36:26–27; Rom. 5:16–17

Kindness Dan. 2:24; Luke 3:3

Knowledge Gen. 32:29; Exod. 19:3; Josh. 4:21–22 (enquiring mind); 1 Kings 4:34 (learning); Ps. 78:4 (education); 103:7; Prov. 22:23; Jer. 22:16 (of God); Dan. 12:5; Matt. 2:2 (of Christ); 19:8 (of sin); Rom. 2:20

Lamb of God Matt. 26:57

Laughter Ps. 77:2; Eccles. 2:1–2

Law Exod. 12:7 (curse of); Prov. 18:18; Isa. 8:16 (testimony of); Matt. 4:4; 5:19; 19:8, 18–19; Acts 16:14 (divine)

Learning (human) Dan. 11:20; Luke 4:4 (of Scriptures); Acts 17:28

Leech Prov. 28:3

Letters (writing) Acts 18:11

Licentiousness Ps. 119:45

Life Ps. 119:17; Lam. 3:39 (with hope); Matt. 6:25 (and livelihood); Acts 11:18 (with repentance); Rom. 14:7–8 (business of our life)

Light Gen. 1:14–19; Job 23:17; Prov. 31:18; Joel 3:15 (of God); Matt. 1:23 (of nature, law & gospel); 4:16; 19:18–19; 24:27 (gospel lightning); 27:45 (of the world); John 12:48 (dispensation of); Acts 16:14 (divine)

Lips Ps. 71:23–24 (rejoicing)

Litigation Matt. 5:38–42

Loaves John 6:26

Logic Job 35:10

London Zech. 2:4

Looking back Gen. 19:26

Genesis to Deuteronomy

Genesis

1:1 Let our make and place, as men, remind us of our duty as Christians, which is always to keep heaven in our eye and the earth under our feet.

Atheism is folly, and atheists are the greatest fools in nature; for they see there is a world that could not make itself, and yet they will not own there is a God that made it.

1:6 What God requires of us he himself works in us, or it is not done.

1:14–19 The lights of heaven are made to serve us, and they do it faithfully, and shine in their season, without fail: but we are set as lights in this world to serve God; and do we in like manner answer the end of our creation? No, we do not, our light does not shine before God as his lights shine before us (Matt. 5:14). We burn our Master's candles, but do not mind our Master's work.

1:26 Let him rule man who said, *Let us make man*.

1:27 How is this image of God upon man defaced! How small are the remains of it, and how great the ruins of it! The Lord renew it upon our souls by his sanctifying grace!

1:29 If God give us food for our lives, let us not, with murmuring Israel, ask food for our lusts (Ps. 78:18; Dan. 1:15).

1:30 He that feeds his birds will not starve his babes.

1:31 Omniscience cannot be separated from omnipotence.

2:8 As clothes came in with sin, so did houses. The heaven was the roof of Adam's house, and never was any roof so curiously ceiled and painted. The earth was his floor, and never was any floor so richly inlaid. The shadow of the trees was his retirement; under them were his dining rooms, his lodging rooms, and never were any rooms so finely hung as these.

2:15 As we are not allowed to be idle in this world, and to do nothing, so we are not allowed to be wilful, and do what we please.

2:21–23 That the woman was *made of a rib out of the side of Adam*; not made out of his head to rule over him, nor out of his feet to be trampled upon by him, but out of his side to be equal with him, under his arm to be protected, and near his heart to be beloved.

3:1 Many a dangerous temptation comes to us in gay fine colours that are but skin-deep, and seems to come from above; for Satan can seem an angel of light.

3:6 The way of sin is downhill; a man cannot stop himself when he will.

3:16 No marvel that our sorrows are multiplied when our sins are: both are innumerable evils.

3:19 If Adam had not sinned, he had not sweated. Let not us, by inordinate care and labour, make our punishment heavier than God has made it; but rather study to lighten our burden, and wipe off our sweat, by eyeing Providence in all and expecting rest shortly.

3:21 Adam and Eve made for themselves aprons of fig-leaves, a covering too narrow for them to *wrap themselves in* (Isa. 28:20). Such are all the rags of our own righteousness. But God made them coats of skins, large, and strong, and durable, and fit for them; such is the righteousness of Christ. Therefore *put on the Lord Jesus Christ*.

4:2 Parents ought to bring up their children to business. 'Give them a Bible and a calling (said good Mr Dod), and God be with them.' Note, That calling or condition of life is best for us, and to be chosen by us, which is best for our souls, that which least exposes us to sin and gives us most opportunity of serving and enjoying God.

4:7 'Now that anger is in thy heart, murder is at the door.'

4:20–22 Here were devices how to be rich, and how to be mighty, and how to be merry, but nothing of God, nor of his fear and service, among them. Present things fill the heads of most people.

4:25 Thus we are *baptized for the dead* (1 Cor. 15:29), that is, we are, by baptism, admitted into the church, for or instead of those who by death, especially by martyrdom, are removed out of it; and we fill up their room.

5:2 *Adam* signifies *earth*, *red earth*. He gave this name both to the man and to the woman. Being at first one by nature, and afterwards one by marriage, it was fit they should both have the same name, in token of their union. The woman is *of the earth earthy* as well as the man.

5:3 Grace does not run in the blood, but corruption does. A sinner begets a sinner, but a saint does not beget a saint.

5:23–24 God often takes those soonest whom he loves best, and the time they lose on earth is gained in heaven, to their unspeakable advantage. Those whose conversation in the world is truly holy shall find their removal out of it truly happy.

6:7 None are ruined by the justice of God but those that hate to be reformed by the grace of God.

6:14 If God gives us habitations that are safe, and warm, and wholesome, we are bound to be thankful, though they are not magnificent or nice.

7:1 Those that keep themselves pure in times of common iniquity God will keep safe in times of common calamity.

7:12 God made the world in six days, but he was forty days in destroying it; for he is slow to anger: but, though the destruction came slowly and gradually, yet it came effectually.

7:16 Those that by faith come into Christ, the ark, shall by the power of God be shut in, and kept as in a stronghold *by the power of God* (1 Peter 1:5) ... There is room enough in Christ for all comers.

7:17 Sanctified afflictions are spiritual promotions; and as troubles abound consolations much more abound.

8:11 The olive-branch, which was an emblem of peace, was brought not by the raven, a bird of prey, nor by a gay and proud peacock, but by a mild, patient, humble, dove. It is a dove-like disposition that brings into the soul earnests of rest and joy. In the fullness of time, God sent forth his gospel, as the dove, in the likeness of which the Holy Spirit descended, and this presents us with an olive-branch and brings in a better hope.

8:20 Noah was now turned out into a cold and desolate world, where one would have thought his first care would have been to build a house for himself; but, behold, he begins with an altar for God: God, that is the first, must be first served; and he begins well that begins with God.

8:21 Man's nature was as sinful after the deluge as it had been before.

8:22 His reasons of mercy are all drawn from himself, not from any thing in us.

9:5 Our lives are not so our own as that we may quit them at our own pleasure, but they are God's, and we must resign them at his pleasure; if we in any way hasten our own deaths, we are accountable to God for it.

9:13 The rainbow has fiery colours in it, to signify that though God will not again drown the world, yet, when the mystery of God shall be finished, the world shall be consumed by fire.

9:27 It is better to dwell in tents with God than in palaces without him. In Salem, where is God's tabernacle, there is more satisfaction than in all the isles of the Gentiles.

10:21 Abraham and his seed, God's covenant-people, not only descended from Heber, but from him were called *Hebrews* (14:13) *Abram the Hebrew*.

11:6 While the builders of Babel, though of different families, dispositions and interests, were thus unanimous in opposing God, what a pity is it, and what a shame, that the builders of Sion, though united in one common head and Spirit, should be divided, as they are, in serving God!

12:5 That which we undertake in obedience to God's command, and a humble attendance upon his providence, will certainly succeed, and end with comfort at last.

12:7 Wherever we go, let us not fail to take our religion along with us.

13:2 There is a burden of care in getting them, fear in keeping them, temptation in using them, guilt in abusing them, sorrow in losing them, and a burden of account, at last, to be given up concerning them. Great possessions do but make men heavy and unwieldy.

As piety is a friend to outward prosperity (1 Tim. 4:8), so outward prosperity, if well managed, is an ornament to piety, and furnishes an opportunity of doing so much the more good.

13:10–11 Sensual choices are sinful choices, and seldom speed well.

13:14–15 Lot had the paradise, such as it was, but Abram had the promise.

14:12 It is just with God to deprive us of those enjoyments by which we have suffered ourselves to be deprived of our enjoyment of him.

14:14 Though our holy religion teaches us to be for peace, yet it does not forbid us to provide for war. Religion tends to make men, not cowardly, but truly valiant. The true Christian is the true hero.

14:20 God must always have his dues out of our substance, especially when by any particular providence, he has either preserved or increased it to us. The tenth of our increase is a very fit proportion to be set apart for the honour of God and the service of his sanctuary.

15:2–3 While promised mercies are delayed our unbelief and impatience are apt to conclude them denied. True believers sometimes find it hard to reconcile God's promises and his providences, when they seem to disagree.

15:12 Holy fear prepares the soul for holy joy; the spirit of bondage makes way for the spirit of adoption. God wounds first, and then heals; humbles first, and then lifts up (Isa. 6:5–6).

15:15 Old age is a blessing. It is promised in the fifth commandment; it is pleasing to nature; and it affords a great opportunity for usefulness.

16:5 When passion is upon the throne, reason is out of doors.

16:8 Those who are forsaking God and their duty would do well to remember not only *whence they have fallen*, but *whither they are falling*.

16:12 Those that have turbulent spirits have commonly troublesome lives.

17:1 I know no religion but sincerity.

18:6–8 Let us be thankful for food convenient, though it be homely and common; and not be desirous of dainties, for they are deceitful meat to those that love them and set their hearts upon them.

18:9 Those are most likely to receive comfort from God and his promises that are in their place and in the way of their duty (Luke 2:8).

18:12 Take notice of what is spoken decently and well, to the honour of those that speak it, though it may be mixed with that which is amiss, over which we should cast a mantle of love.

18:32 We cannot expect too little from man nor too much from God.

19:26 The pillar of salt should season us. Since it is such a dangerous thing to look back, let us always press forward (Phil. 3:13–14).

19:27 We must direct our prayer as a letter, and then look up for an answer, direct our prayer as an arrow, and then look up to see whether it reach the mark.

20:3 Every wilful sinner ought to be told that he is a dead man, as the condemned malefactor, and the patient whose disease is mortal, are said to be so. If thou art a bad man, certainly thou art a dead man.

22:5 It is our wisdom and duty, when we are going to worship God, to lay aside all those thoughts and cares which may divert us from the service, [and] leave them at the bottom of the hill, that we may attend on the Lord without distraction.

22:12 Our creature-comforts are most likely to be continued to us when we are most willing to resign them up to God's will.

22:13–14 It is observable that the temple, the place of sacrifice, was afterwards built upon this mount Moriah (2 Chr. 3:1), and mount Calvary, where Christ was crucified, was not far off.

23:1 Old people will die never the sooner, but may die the better, for reckoning themselves old.

23:2 Tears are a tribute due to our deceased friends. When the body is sown, it must be watered.

24:12–14 It is our wisdom, in all our affairs, to follow Providence, and folly to force it. It is very desirable, and that which we may lawfully pray for, while in the general we set God's will before us as our rule, that he will, by hints of providence, direct us in the way of our duty, and give us indications what his mind is.

24:12 What we win by prayer we must wear with praise; for mercies in answer to prayer lay us under particular obligations.

24:21 Providence sometimes wonderfully directs those that by faith and prayer seek direction from heaven in the choice of suitable yoke-fellows: happy marriages those are likely to be that are made in the fear of God; and these, we are sure, are made in heaven.

24:63 Holy souls love retirement. It will do us good to be often left alone, walking alone and sitting alone; and, if we have the art of improving solitude, we shall find we are never less alone than when alone.

25:5–6 In many cases it is wisdom for men to make their own hands their executors, and what they find to do to do it while they live, as far as they can.

25:8 A good man, though he should not die old, dies full of days, satisfied with living here, and longing to live in a better place.

25:10 Those that in life have been very dear to each other may not only innocently, but laudably, desire to be buried together, that in their deaths they may not be divided, and in token of their hopes of rising together.

25:22 The word and prayer, by both which we now enquire of the Lord, give great relief to those that are upon any account perplexed. It is a great relief to the mind to spread our case before the Lord, and ask counsel at his mouth.

25:30 Those that addict themselves to sport *weary themselves for very vanity* (Hab. 2:13). They might do the most needful business, and gain the greatest advantages, with half the pains they take, and half the perils they run into, in pursuit of their foolish pleasures.

25:33 God often chooses the foolish things of the world, by them to confound the wise. Plain Jacob makes a fool of cunning Esau.

26:2–3 As we may go any where with comfort when God's blessing goes with us, so we may stay any where contentedly if that blessing rest upon us.

26:24 Those may remove with comfort that are sure of God's presence with them wherever they go.

28:12 The angels are active spirits, continually ascending and descending; they rest not, day nor night, from service, according to the posts assigned them. They ascend to give account of what they have done, and to receive orders; and then descend, to execute the orders they have received. Thus we should always abound in the work of the Lord, that we may do it as the angels do it (Ps. 103:20–21).

30:2 Sometimes it is requisite that a reproof should be given warm, like a medical potion; not too hot, lest it scald the patient; yet not too cold, lest it prove ineffectual.

30:25–26 Those that trust in God, in his providence and promise, though they have great families and small incomes, can cheerfully hope that he who sends mouths will send meat. He who feeds the brood of the ravens will not starve the seed of the righteous.

30:30 Faith and charity, though they are excellent things, must not take us off from making necessary provision for our own support, and the support of our families.

31:4 Husbands that love their wives will communicate their purposes and intentions to them. Where there is a mutual affection there will be a mutual confidence. And the prudence of the wife should engage the heart of her husband to trust in her (Prov. 31:11).

31:30 Happy are those who have the Lord for their God, for they have a God that they cannot be robbed of. Enemies may steel our goods, but not our God.

31:44 When quarrels happen, we should be willing to be friends again upon any terms: peace and love are such valuable jewels that we can scarcely buy them too dearly. Better sit down losers than go on in strife.

31:53 Those that have one God should have one heart: those that agree in religion should strive to agree in everything else.

32:1–2 A good man may with an eye of faith see the same that Jacob saw with his bodily eyes, by believing that promise (Ps. 91:11), *He shall give his angels charge over thee.* What need have we to dispute whether every particular saint has a guardian angel, when we are sure he has a guard of angels about him?

32:6 Angry men have good memories.

32:9 Jacob had lately seen his guard of angels, but, in this distress, he applied to God, not to them; he knew they were his fellow-servants (Rev. 22:9).

32:11 Natural affection may furnish us with allowable acceptable pleas in prayer.

32:13 We must so depend upon God's providence as to make use of our own prudence. 'Help thyself, and God will help thee.'

32:29 The tree of life is better than the tree of knowledge.

33:3 Many preserve themselves by humbling themselves: the bullet flies over him that stoops.

33:12–14 There may be those with whom we cannot fall in and yet with whom we need not fall out by the way.

33:17–20 Where we have a tent God must have an altar; where we have a house he must have a church in it.

34:5 Things never go well when the authority of a parent runs low in a family. Let every man *bear rule in his own house, and have his children in subjection with all gravity*.

34:30 When sin is in the house, there is reason to fear ruin at the door.

35:7 The comfort which the saints have in holy ordinances is not as much from *Bethel, the house of God*, as from *El-beth-el*, *the God of the house*. The ordinances are but empty things if we do not meet with God in them.

35:9 God will appear to those in a way of grace that attend on him in a way of duty.

35:19 If the soul be at rest after death, it matters little where the body lies. In the place where the tree falls, there let it lie.

36:15–19 Edomites may be dukes with men, but Israelites indeed are made to our God kings and priests.

36:43 The children of this world have their all in hand, and nothing in hope (Luke 16:25); while the children of God have their all in hope, and next to nothing in hand. But, all things considered, it is better to have Canaan in promise than mount Seir in possession.

37:2 Those that are trained up to do nothing are likely to be good for nothing.

37:23–24 God's providences often seem to contradict his purposes, even when they are serving them, and working at a distance towards the accomplishment of them.

37:28 As Joseph was sold by the contrivance of Judah for twenty pieces of silver, so was our Lord Jesus for thirty, and by one of the same name too, *Judas*.

37:31–32 They sent him Joseph's coat of many colours, with one colour more than it had had, a bloody colour.

37:35 Inordinate love commonly ends in immoderate grief; as much as the sway of the pendulum throws one way, so much it will throw the other way. We often perplex ourselves with imaginary troubles.

38:23 There are many who are more solicitous to preserve their reputation with men than to secure the favour of God and a good conscience; *lest we be shamed* goes further with them than *lest we be damned*.

39:9 Gracious souls look upon this as the worst thing in sin that it is against God, against his nature and his dominion, against his love and his design. Those that love God do for this reason hate sin.

39:10–12 Those that would be kept from harm must keep themselves out of harm's way.

39:18 This was not the first time that Joseph's coat was used as a false witness concerning him; his father had been deceived by it before, now his master.

40:1 High places are slippery places; nothing more uncertain than the favour of princes.

40:19 Ministers are but interpreters; they cannot make things otherwise than it is.

40:20 We may all profitably take notice of our birth-days, with thankfulness for the mercies of our birth, sorrow for the sinfulness of it, and an expectation of the day of our death as better than the day of our birth.

43:11 It is no fault, but our wisdom and duty, to alter our purposes and resolutions when there is a good reason for our so doing. Constancy is a virtue, but obstinacy is not.

47:5–6 Whatever our profession or employment is, we should aim to be excellent in it, and to prove ourselves ingenious and industrious.

48:1 The sick bed is a proper place both for giving comfort and counsel to others and receiving instruction ourselves. It is good to acquaint young people that are coming into the world with the aged servants of God that are going out of it, whose dying testimony to the goodness of God, and the pleasantness of wisdom's ways, may be a great encouragement to the rising generation.

48:7 Strong affections in the enjoyment cause long affliction in the loss.

49:5–7 We ought always, in the expressions of our zeal, carefully to distinguish between the sinner and the sin, so as not to love nor bless the sin for the sake of the person, nor to hate nor curse the person for the sake of the sin.

49:13 God appoints the bounds of our habitation. It is our wisdom and duty to accommodate ourselves to our lot and to improve it.

49:18 Christ, as our way to heaven, is to be waited on; and heaven, as our rest in Christ, is to be waited for.

50:15 Those that would be fearless must keep themselves guiltless.

Exodus

2:2 When men are projecting the church's ruin God is preparing for its salvation.

2:4 Duty is ours, events are God's.

3:12 Those that are weak in themselves may yet do wonders, being strong in the Lord and in the power of his might; and those that are most diffident of themselves may be most confident in God.

3:14 The greatest and best man in the world must say, By the grace of God *I am what I am*; but God says absolutely—and it is more than any creature, man or angel, can say—*I am that I am*. Being self-existent, he cannot but be self-sufficient, and therefore all-sufficient, and the inexhaustible fountain of being and bliss.

4:10 A great deal of wisdom and true worth is concealed by a slow tongue. Christ's disciples were no orators, till the Spirit made them such.

4:22 *Thus saith the Lord;* this is the first time *that* preface is used by any man which afterwards is used so frequently by all the prophets: whether Pharaoh will hear, or whether he will forbear, Moses must tell him, *Thus saith the Lord*.

4:24, 26 Solitude has its advantages, but they seldom counterbalance the loss of Christian communion.

4:27–28 Those that are fellow-servants to God in the same work should use a mutual freedom, and endeavour rightly and fully to understand one another.

5:9 The malice of Satan has often represented the service and worship of God as fit employment for those only that have nothing else to do, and the business only of the idle; whereas indeed it is the indispensable duty of those that are most busy in the world.

5:14 The lowest ebbs go before the highest tides; and very cloudy mornings commonly introduce the fairest days (Deut. 32:36). God's time to help is when things are at the worst; and Providence verifies the paradox, *The worse the better*.

5:17 It is well for us that men are not to be our judges, but a God who knows what the principles are on which we act.

6:1 Man's extremity is God's opportunity of helping and saving.

6:3 God would now be known by his name *Jehovah*, that is, (1.) A God performing what he had promised, and so inspiring confidence in his promises. (2.) A God perfecting what he had begun, and finishing his own work. In the history of the creation, God is never called Jehovah till the heavens and the earth were finished (Gen. 2:4).

6:9 Strong passions oppose strong consolations. By indulging ourselves in discontent and fretfulness, we deprive ourselves of the comfort we might have both from God's word and from his providence, and must thank ourselves if we go comfortless.

7:20 One of the first miracles Moses wrought was turning water into blood, but one of the first miracles our Lord Jesus wrought was turning water into wine; for the law was given by Moses, and it was a dispensation of death and terror; but grace and truth, which like wine, make glad the heart, came by Jesus Christ.

8:23 The Lord knows those that are his, and will make it appear, perhaps in this world, certainly in the other, that he has set them apart for himself.

9:29 Even those whom we have little hopes of, yet we should continue to pray for, and to admonish (1 Sam. 12:23).

9:34–35 Little credit is to be given to confessions upon the rack.

10:18–19 Whatever point of the compass the wind is in, it is fulfilling God's word, and turns about by his counsel.

10:22–23 Spiritual darkness is spiritual bondage; while Satan blinds men's eyes that they see not, he binds their hands and feet that they work not for God, nor move towards heaven.

Let us dread the consequences of sin; if three days' darkness was so dreadful, what will everlasting darkness be?

11:8 It is a great vexation to the spirits of good ministers to see people deaf to all the fair warnings given them, and running headlong into ruin, notwithstanding all the kind methods taken to prevent it. To be angry at nothing but sin is the way not to sin in anger.

12:3, 6 It is very observable that as Christ was crucified at the Passover, so he solemnly entered into Jerusalem four days before, the very day that the paschal lamb was set apart.

12:7 If the blood of Christ be sprinkled upon our consciences, it will be our protection from the wrath of God, the curse of the law and the damnation of hell (Rom. 8:1).

12:8 We must feed upon Christ with sorrow and brokenness of heart, in remembrance of sin; this will give an admirable relish to the paschal lamb.

Christ will be sweet to us if sin be bitter.

12:13 In times of common calamity God will secure his own people, and set a mark upon them; they shall be hidden either in heaven or under heaven, preserved either from the stroke of judgments or at least from the sting of them.

13:14 God's service is reasonable, and it is then acceptable when we perform it intelligently, knowing what we do and why we do it.

13:17–18 Man proposes, but God disposes, and in his disposal we must acquiesce, and set ourselves to follow providence.

13:22 The children of Israel were baptized unto Moses in this cloud, which, some think, distilled dew upon them (1 Cor. 10:2).

14:11 As the Egyptians were angry with themselves for the best deed they ever did, so the Israelites were angry with God for the greatest kindness that was ever done them; so gross are the absurdities of unbelief.

15:25 Some make this tree typical of the cross of Christ, which sweetens the bitter waters of affliction to all the faithful, and enables them to rejoice in tribulation.

16:10 What God's ministers say to us is then likely to do us good when the glory of God shines in with it upon our souls.

16:16 What God graciously gives we must industriously gather; with quietness working, and eating our own bread, not the bread either of idleness or deceit.

17:6 The pleasures of sense are puddle-water; spiritual delights are rock-water, so pure, so clear, so refreshing—rivers of pleasure.

17:12 We should not be shy either of asking help from others or giving help to others, for we are members one of another.

18:17 There may be over-doing even in well-doing, and therefore our zeal must always be governed by discretion, that our good may not be evil spoken of.

19:3 In all our dealings with God, free grace anticipates us with the blessings of goodness, and all our comfort is owing, not to our knowing God, but rather to our being *known of him* (Gal. 4:9).

20:12 Those that do their duty to their parents are most likely to have the comfort of that which their parents gather for them and leave to them; those that support their parents shall find that God, the common Father, will support them.

20:14 Our chastity should be as dear to us as our lives, and we should be as much afraid of that which defiles the body as of that which destroys it.

20:24–25 The beauty of holiness needs no paint.

23:10–11 If we are prudent and diligent in our affairs, we may trust Providence to furnish us with the bread of the day in its day.

23:30 God, in his providence, often delays mercies, because we are not ready for them.

24:10 They saw the God of Israel, that is, they had some glimpse of his glory, in light and fire, though they saw *no manner of similitude*. Nothing is described but that which was under his feet; for our conceptions of God are all below him, and fall infinitely short of being adequate.

24:16 Communion with God is worth waiting for, and it is fit we should address ourselves to solemn ordinances with a solemn pause, taking time to compose ourselves (Ps. 108:1).

25:9 He that gave us no account of the lines and circles of the globe, the diameter of the earth, or the height and magnitude of the stars, has told us particularly the measure of every board and curtain of the tabernacle; for God's church and instituted religion are more precious to him and more considerable than all the rest of the world.

26:6 There were to be two hangings, five breadths in each, sewed together, and the two hangings coupled together with golden clasps, or tacks, so that it might be all one tabernacle. Thus the churches of Christ and the saints, though they are many, are yet one, being *fitly joined together* in holy love, and by the *unity of the Spirit*, so growing into one *holy temple* in *the Lord* (Eph. 2:21–22; 4:16).

28:1 A blessed thing it is when real holiness goes, as the ceremonial holiness did, by succession in a family.

28:29 How near should Christ's name be to our hearts, since he is pleased to lay our names so near his! And what a comfort it is to us, in all our addresses to God, that the great high priest of our profession has the names of all his Israel upon his breast before the Lord *for a memorial*, presenting them to God as the people of his choice, who were to be made *accepted in the beloved!*

29:9 They [ministers] cannot fill the people's hearts unless God fill their hands; to him therefore they must go, and *receive from his fulness*.

29:35 Gospel ministers are to be solemnly set apart to the work of the ministry with great deliberation and seriousness both in the ordainers and in the ordained, as those that are to be employed in a great work and entrusted with a great charge.

29:38–39 Our daily devotions must be looked upon as the most needful of our daily works and the most pleasant of our daily comforts. Whatever business we have, this must never be omitted, either morning or evening; prayer-time must be kept up as duly as meat-time. Those starve their own souls that keep not up a constant attendance on the throne of grace.

29:45–46 Those are truly happy that have a covenant-interest in God as theirs and the comfortable evidence of that interest. If we have this, we have enough, and need no more to make us happy.

30:36 The incense which was burned upon the golden altar … when it was used, it was to be beaten very small: thus it pleased the Lord to bruise the Redeemer when he offered himself for a sacrifice of a sweet-smelling savour.

31:6 Skill in common arts and employments is the gift of God; from him are derived both the faculty and the improvement of the faculty.

32:3 Shall we grudge the expenses of our religion, or starve so good a cause?

32:13 God's promises are to be our pleas in prayer; for what he has promised he is able to perform, and the honour of this truth is engaged for the performance of it.

32:30–31 The work of ministers is to show people their sins, and the greatness of their sins. Thus men's sins and their follies make work for their friends and ministers, unpleasant work, many times, and give great interruptions to that work which they delight in.

33:15–16 Those who know how to value God's favours are best prepared to receive them. God's special presence with us in this wilderness, by his Spirit and grace, to direct, defend and comfort us, is the surest pledge of his special love to us and will redound to his glory as well as our benefit.

33:19 All his reasons of mercy are fetched from within himself, not from any merit in his creatures: as he has mercy on whom he will, so, because he will. *Even so, Father, because it seemed good in thy sight*. It is never said, 'I will be angry at whom I will be angry,' for his wrath is always just and holy; but *I will show mercy on whom I will show mercy*, for his grace is always free. He never damns by prerogative, but by prerogative he saves. The apostle quotes this (Rom. 9:15) in answer to those who charged God with unrighteousness in giving that grace freely to some which he withholds justly from others.

34:14 Those cannot worship God aright who do not worship him alone.

Leviticus

6:28 The vessel in which the flesh of the sin-offering was boiled must be broken if it were an earthen one, and, if a brazen one, well washed. This intimated that the defilement was not wholly taken away by the offering, but did rather cleave to it, such was the weakness and deficiency of those sacrifices; but the blood of Christ thoroughly cleanses from all sin (1 John 1:7), and after it there needs no cleansing.

8:35–36 Gospel ministers are compared to those who served at the altar, for they *minister about holy things* (1 Cor. 9:13), they are God's mouth to the people and the people's to God, the pastors and teachers Christ has appointed to continue in the church to the end of the world: they seem to be meant in that promise which points at gospel times (Isa. 66:21), *I will take of them for priests and for Levites.* No man may take this honour to himself, but he who upon trial is found to be clothed and anointed by the Spirit of God with gifts and graces to qualify him for it, and who with purpose of heart devotes himself entirely to the service, and is then by the *word and prayer* (for so every thing is sanctified), and the imposition of the hands of those that *give themselves to the word and prayer* (Acts 6:4), set apart to the office, and recommended to Christ as a servant and to the church as a steward and guide. And those that are thus solemnly dedicated to God ought not to depart from his service, but faithfully to abide in it all their days; and those that do so, and continue *labouring in the word and doctrine*, are to be accounted *worthy of double honour* (1 Tim. 5:17), double to that of the Old Testament priests.

9:22 Aaron, when he had blessed, came down; Christ, when he blessed, went up.

22:17–18 If our devotions are ignorant, and cold, and trifling, and full of distractions, we offer *the lame, and the sick, for sacrifice*; but cursed be the deceiver that does so, for, while he thinks to put a cheat upon God, he puts a damning cheat upon his own soul.

23:12 It is very observable that our Lord Jesus rose from the dead on the very day that the first-fruits were offered, to show that he was the substance of this shadow.

23:14 We must always begin with God, begin our lives with him, begin every day with him, begin every meal with him, begin every affair and business with him; *seek first the kingdom of God*.

23:40–42 The tradition of the Jews is that they were to express their joy by dancing, and singing hymns of praise to God, with musical instruments: and not the common people only, but the wise men of Israel, and their elders, were to do it in the court of the sanctuary: for (they say) the joy with which a man rejoices in doing a commandment is really a great service.

Numbers

10:36 The welfare and happiness of the Israel of God consist in the continual presence of God among them. Their safety consists not in their numbers, though they are thousands, many thousands, but in the favour of God, and his gracious return to them and residence with them.

11:29 We must not be forward to condemn and silence those that differ from us, as if they did not follow Christ because they do not follow *him with us* (Mark 9:38). Shall we reject those whom Christ has owned, or restrain any from doing good because they are not in every thing of our mind? Moses was of another spirit; so far from silencing these two, and quenching the Spirit in them, he wishes *all the Lord's people were prophets*, that is, he would *put his Spirit upon them*. Not that he would have any set up for prophets that were not duly qualified, or that he expected that the Spirit of prophecy should be made thus common; but thus he expresses the love and esteem he had for *all the Lord's people* … such an excellent spirit as this blessed Paul was of, rejoicing that Christ was preached, though it was by those who therein intended to *add affliction to his bonds* (Phil. 1:16).

14:1 Unbelief, or distrust of God, is a sin that is its own punishment.

15:40 That great and fundamental law of religion [is], *Be holy unto your God,* purged from sin, and sincerely devoted to his service.

16:33 Others' ruins should be our warnings. Could we by faith hear the outcries of those that have gone down to the bottomless pit, we should give more diligence than we do to escape for our lives, lest we also come into that condemnation.

18:19 Thus provision is made that a gospel ministry should continue till Christ comes, by an ordinance for ever. *Lo, I am with you* (that is their maintenance and support) *always, even to the end of the world* (Matt. 28:20). Thanks be to the Redeemer, it is the word which he has *commanded to a thousand generations.*

20:28 Death will strip us; naked we came into the world, and naked we must go out. We shall see little reason to be proud of our clothes, our ornaments, or marks of honour, if we consider how soon death will strip us of our glory, divest us of all our offices and honours, and take the crown off from our head.

29:11 Though we must not repent that we have repented, yet we must repent that we have not repented better. It likewise intimated the imperfection of the legal sacrifices, and their insufficiency to take away sin, that on the very day the *sin-offering of atonement* was offered, yet there must be another sin-offering. But *what the law could not do, in that it was weak*, that Christ has done (Rom. 8:3).

32:14 If men did but consider, as they ought, what would be the end of sin, they would be afraid of the beginnings of it.

36:13 Whatever new condition God is by his providence bringing us into, we must beg of him to teach us the duty of it, and to enable us to do it, that we may do the work of the day in its day, of the place in its place.

Deuteronomy

3:20 We are not born for ourselves, but are members one of another.

3:28 Those to whom God gives a charge, he will be sure to give encouragement to. And it is a comfort to the church's friends (when they are dying and going off) to see God's work likely to be carried on by other hands, when they are silent in the dust.

6:5 Did ever any prince make a law that his subjects should love him? Yet such is the condescension of the divine grace that this is made the first and great commandment of God's law, that we love him, and that we perform all other parts of our duty to him from a principle of love.

6:6 He that loves God loves his Bible.

7:1–2 The confining of this commission to the nations here mentioned plainly intimates that after-ages were not to draw this into a precedent; this will not serve to justify those barbarous laws which give no quarter.

8:3 God often brings his people low, that he may have the honour of helping them.

8:10 From all our comfortable enjoyments we must take occasion to thank God for our comfortable settlements; and I know not but we of this nation have as much reason as they to give thanks for a good land.

11:10–12 The better God has provided, by our outward condition, for our ease and convenience, the more we should abound in his service: the less we have to do for our bodies the more we should do for God and our souls.

20:19–20 Christ took care that the broken meat should be gathered up, that nothing might be lost. Every creature of God is good, and, as nothing is to be refused, so nothing is to be abused. We may live to want what we carelessly waste.

21:17 No son should be abandoned by his father till he manifestly appear to be abandoned of God, which is hard to say of any while there is life.

30:1 Consideration is the first step towards conversion.

31:11 It is the will of God that all people should acquaint themselves with his word. It is a rule to all, and therefore should be read to all.

34:5 The servants of the Lord, when they have done all their other work, must die at last, in obedience to their Master, and be freely willing to go home whenever he sends for them (Acts 21:13).

34:8 If we hope to go to heaven rejoicing, why should we resolve to go to the grave mourning? The ceremonial law of Moses is dead and buried in the grave of Christ; but the Jews have not yet ended the days of their mourning for it.

34:10 Moses was faithful as a servant, but Christ as a Son. The history of Moses leaves him buried in the plains of Moab, and concludes with the period of his government; but the history of our Saviour leaves him sitting *at the right hand of the majesty on high*, and we are assured that *of the increase of his government and peace there shall be no end*.

Joshua to 1 Kings

Joshua

Preface p. iii If I may but be instrumental to make my readers wise and good, wiser and better, more watchful against sin and more careful of their duty both to God and man, and, in order thereto, more in love with the word and law of God, I have all I desire, all I aim at.

1:7–8 It is not enough to hear and read the word, to commend and admire it, to know and remember it, to talk and discourse of it, but we must do it.

2:1 We do not trust God, but tempt him, if our expectations slacken our endeavours.

2:19 Those that will be conscientious in keeping their promises will be cautious in making them, and perhaps may insert conditions which others may think frivolous.

3:7 Some have observed that it was at the banks of Jordan that God began to magnify Joshua, and at the same place he began to magnify our Lord Jesus as Mediator; for John was baptizing at Bethabara, *the house of passage*, and there it was that when our Saviour was baptized it was proclaimed concerning him, *This is my beloved Son.*

3:11 While we make God's precepts our rule, his promises our stay, and his providence our guide, we need not dread the greatest difficulties we may meet with in the way of duty.

4:21–22 Those that will be wise when they are old must be inquisitive when they are young. Our Lord Jesus, though he had in himself the fullness of knowledge, has by his example taught children and young people to hear and ask questions, Luke 2:46.

6:5 Thus by faith, not by force, the walls of Jericho fell down.

6:8 Thus by the foolishness of preaching, fitly compared to the sounding of these rams' horns, the devil's kingdom is thrown down; and the *weapons of our warfare*, though they are not carnal nor seem to a carnal eye likely to bring anything to pass, are yet *mighty through God to the pulling down of strongholds*, 2 Cor. 10:4–5.

6:19 God had promised them a land *flowing with milk and honey*, not a land abounding with silver and gold; for he would have them live comfortably in it, that they might serve him cheerfully, but not covet either to trade with distant countries or to hoard for after times.

8:15 So our Lord Jesus, when he bowed his head and gave up the ghost, seemed as if death had triumphed over him, and as if he and all his interests had been routed and ruined; but in his resurrection he rallied again and gave the powers of darkness a total defeat; he broke the serpent's head, by suffering him to bruise his heel. A glorious stratagem!

9:15 We make more haste than good speed in any business when we stay not to take God along with us, and by the word and prayer to consult him. Would we acknowledge him in all our ways, we should find them more safe, easy and successful.

9:16 A lying tongue is but for a moment, and truth will be the daughter of time.

9:20 We must never be overawed, either by majesty or multitude, to do a sinful thing, and go against our consciences.

9:22 Under the greatest provocations, it is our wisdom and duty to keep our temper, and to bridle our passion; a just cause needs not anger to defend it, and a bad one is made never the better by it.

11:21 God sometimes reserves the sharpest trials of his people by afflictions and temptation for the latter end of their days. Therefore *let not him that girds on the harness boast as he* *that puts it off*. Death, that tremendous son of Anak, is the last enemy that is to be encountered, but it is *to be destroyed*, 1 Cor. 15:26. Thanks be to God who will give us the victory.

14:10 While we live, it is God that keeps us alive; by his power he protects us from death, and by his bounty supplies us continually with the supports and comforts of life. He *holdeth our soul in life*.

15:16 Let us learn hence not to seek and mind our own things only, but to concern and engage ourselves for the welfare of the community we are members of; we are not born for ourselves, nor must we *live to ourselves*.

15:19 From this story we learn (1.) That it is no breach of the tenth commandment moderately to desire those comforts and conveniences of this life which we see attainable in a fair and regular way. (2.) That husbands and wives should mutually advise, and jointly agree, about that which is for the common good of their family; and much more should they concur in asking of their heavenly Father the best blessings, those of the upper springs. (3.) That parents must never think that lost which is bestowed upon their children for their real advantage, but must be free in giving them portions as well as maintenance, especially when they are dutiful.

17:16–18 We straiten ourselves by apprehending the difficulties in the way of our enlargement to be greater than really they are. What can be insuperable to faith and holy resolution?

18:9 What we have in the world we must acknowledge God's property in, and dispose of it as before him, with justice, and charity, and dependence upon Providence. The heavenly Canaan is described to us in a book, the book of the scriptures, and there are in it mansions and portions sufficient for all God's spiritual Israel. Christ is our Joshua that divides it to us. On him we must attend, and to him we must apply for an inheritance with the saints in light. See John 17:2–3.

19:9 It is good being in a good neighbourhood.

20:2 God's spiritual Israel have and shall have, in Christ and heaven, not only rest to repose themselves in, but refuge to secure themselves in.

21:1–8 There is a particular providence directing and attending the removals and settlements of ministers, and appointing where those shall fix who are to be the lights of the world.

22:4, 9 Though masters of families may sometimes have occasion to be absent, long absent, from their families, yet, when their business abroad is finished, they must remember home is their place, from which they ought not to wander as a bird from her nest.

23:2 When we see death hastening towards us, this should quicken us to do the work of life with all our might.

23:8 The way to make people better is to make the best of them.

23:14; 24:1 We must never think our work for God done till our life is done; and, if he lengthen out our days beyond what we thought, we must conclude it is because he has some further service for us to do.

24:31 While Joshua lived, religion was kept up among them under his care and influence; but soon after he and his contemporaries died it went to decay, so much oftentimes does one head hold up: how well is it for the gospel church that Christ, our Joshua, is still with it, by his Spirit, and will be always, even *unto the end of the world*!

Judges

6:11 We put ourselves in the way of divine visits when we employ ourselves in honest business. Tidings of Christ's birth were brought to the shepherds when they were keeping their flocks.

6:31 Let us do our duty, and then trust God with our safety.

8:2–3 Humility is most amiable and admirable in the midst of great attainments and advancements.

8:7 Many are taught with the briers and thorns of affliction that would not learn otherwise.

9:11 Those who are preferred to places of public trust and power must resolve to forego all their private interests and advantages, and sacrifice them to the good of the community.

9:26 Men of no conscience will be men of no constancy.

10:6 If God have not all the heart, he will soon have none of it.

11:9 The same question is put to those who desire salvation by Christ. If he save you, will you be willing that he shall rule you? for on no other terms will he save you. If he make you happy, shall he make you holy? If he be your helper, shall he be your head?

11:35 From Jephthah's concern on this occasion, we must learn not to think it strange if the day of our triumphs in this world prove upon some account or other the day of our griefs, and therefore must always rejoice with trembling; we hope for a day of triumph hereafter, which will have no alloy.

12:4 It is an ill thing to fasten names or characters of reproach upon persons or countries, as is common, especially upon those that lie under outward disadvantages: it often occasions quarrels that prove of ill consequence, as it did here.

13:2–5 Mercies long waited for often prove signal mercies, and it is made to appear that they were worth waiting for, and by them others may be encouraged to continue their hope in God's mercy.

13:20 Prayer is the ascent of the soul to God. But it is Christ in the heart by faith that makes it an offering of a sweet smelling savour: without him our services are offensive smoke, but in him acceptable flame.

14:3 He that in the choice of a wife is guided only by his eye, and governed by his fancy, must afterwards thank himself if he find a Philistine in his arms.

15:1 When differences happen between near relations, let those be ever reckoned the wisest and the best that are the most forward to forgive and forget injuries and most willing to stoop and yield for peace' sake.

16:28 Samson died praying, so did our blessed Saviour; but Samson prayed for vengeance, Christ for forgiveness.

17:2 Outward losses drive good people to their prayers, but bad people to their curses.

17:10 The ministry is the best calling but the worst trade in the world.

20:25 We may be sure of the righteousness, when we cannot see the reasons, of God's proceedings.

Ruth

1:10–15 Strong passions, without a settled judgment, commonly produce weak resolutions. Thoughts ripened into resolves by serious consideration are likely to be kept always in the imagination of the heart, whereas what is soon ripe is soon rotten.

2:2 A disposition to diligence bodes well both for this world and the other. Love not sleep, love not sport, love not sauntering; but love business.

2:3 Many a great affair is brought about by a little turn, which seemed fortuitous to us, but was directed by Providence with design.

3:11 If poor people be but good people, they shall have honour from God and man.

1 Samuel

1:3–8 If the devotions of a family prevail not to put an end to its divisions, yet let not the divisions put a stop to the devotions.

2:1–2 Every stream should lead us to the fountain; and the favours we receive from God should raise our admiration of the infinite perfections there are in God.

2:20–21 What is lent to the Lord will certainly be repaid with interest, to our unspeakable advantage, and oftentimes in kind. There is nothing lost by lending to God or losing for him; it shall be repaid *a hundredfold*, Matt. 19:29.

4:3 It is common for those that have estranged themselves from the vitals of religion to discover a great fondness for the rituals and external observances of it, for those that even deny the power of godliness not only to have, but to have in admiration, the form of it.

7:10 When we endeavour to give glory to God we may hope he will, in answer to our prayers, work for his own glory.

7:13 Samuel was a protector and deliverer to Israel, not by dint of sword, as Gideon, nor by strength of arm, as Samson, but by the power of prayer to God and carrying on a work of reformation among the people.

8:1 Those that are in the prime of their time ought to be busy in doing the work of life: for, as they go into years, they will find themselves less disposed to it and less able for it.

9:6 There are many that will consult a man of God, if he comes in their way, that would not go a step out of their way to get wisdom.

10:6 Saul, by praising God in the communion of saints, became another man, but whether a new man or no may be questioned.

12:17 We must never think well of that which God in his law frowns upon, though in his providence he may seem to smile upon it.

12:24 The way of duty is the way of pleasure and profit.

14:41 Some have condemned games that depend purely upon lot or chance as making too bold with a sacred thing.

15:6 A good man leaves the divine blessing for an inheritance to his children's children; those that come after us may be reaping the benefit of our good works when we are in our graves.

15:11 Repentance in God is not, as it is in us, a change of his mind, but a change of his method or dispensation. He does not alter his will, but wills an alteration.

16:2 Those that go about God's work in God's way shall be directed step by step, wherever they are at a loss, to do it in the best manner.

16:7 Let us reckon that to be true beauty which is within, and judge of men, as far as we are capable, by their minds, not their mien.

16:13 The best evidence of our being predestinated to the kingdom of glory is our being sealed with the Spirit of promise, and our experience of a work of grace in our own hearts.

16:23 Music has a natural tendency to compose and exhilarate the mind, when it is disturbed and saddened. Elisha used it for the calming of his spirits, 2 Kings 3:15.

17:2 Business is a good antidote against melancholy. Let the mind have something without to fasten on and employ itself about, and it will be the less in danger of preying upon itself.

18:4 Our Lord Jesus has thus shown his love to us, that he stripped himself to clothe us, emptied himself to enrich us; nay, he did more than Jonathan, he clothed himself with our rags, whereas Jonathan did not put on David's.

21:1 It is a great comfort to us in a day of trouble that we have a

God to go to, to whom we may open our case, and from whom we may ask and expect direction.

23:9 We have the scriptures, those lively oracles, in our hands; let us take advice from them in doubtful cases. 'Bring hither the Bible.'

24:5 It is a good thing to have a heart within us smiting us for our sins that seem little; it is a sign that conscience is awake and tender, and will be the means of preventing greater sins.

24:22 God has many ways to tie the hands of persecutors, when he does not turn their hearts.

25:1 Let old people be willing to rest themselves, though it look like burying themselves alive.

25:18 Husbands and wives, for their common good and benefit, have a joint-interest in their worldly possessions; but if either waste, or unduly spend in any way, it is a robbing of the other.

26:19 It should be more comfortable for us to think of God's title to our estates and his interest in them than our own, and that with them we may honour him than that with them we may maintain ourselves.

30:26 Munificence recommends a man more than magnificence.

31:2 We cannot judge of the spiritual or eternal state of any by the manner of their death; for in that *there is one event to the righteous and to the wicked.*

2 Samuel

1:16 We may learn from it that to give assistance to any in murdering themselves, either directly or indirectly, if done wittingly, incurs the guilt of blood, and that the lives of princes ought to be, in a special manner, precious to us.

3:21 Thus it behoves all who fear God and keep his commandments to avoid strife, even with the wicked, to live at peace with all men, and to show the world that they are children of the light.

5:1 Those who take Christ for their king may thus plead with him: '*We are thy bone and thy flesh*, thou hast made thy self in all things *like unto thy brethren* (Heb. 2:17); therefore be thou our ruler, and let this ruin be under thy hand,' Isa. 3:6.

5:24 God's grace must quicken our endeavours. If God work in us both to will and to do, it does not follow that we must sit still, as those that have nothing to do, but we must therefore *work out our own salvation* with all possible care and diligence, Phil. 2:12–13.

6:21 We should be afraid of censuring the devotion of others though it may not agree with our sentiments, because, for aught that we know, the heart may be upright in it, and who are we that we should despise those whom God has accepted?

7:18 What God has laid out upon his people is much, but what he has laid up for them is infinitely more, Ps. 31:19.

10:14 It is one thing when men may either fight or fly and another thing when they must either fight or die.

11:1 When we are out of the way of our duty, we are in the way of temptation.

12:1 Though God may suffer his people to fall into sin, he will not suffer them to lie still in it.

12:20 Weeping must never hinder worshipping.

13:2 Grace does not run in the blood, but corruption does.

14:11 Nothing is more proper, nor more powerful, to engage us to every duty, especially to all acts of mercy and kindness, than to remember the Lord our God.

14:21 God's laws were never designed to be like cobwebs, which catch the little flies, but suffer the great ones to break through.

16:5 The world's smiles are more dangerous than its frowns.

17:23 That will break a proud man's heart that will not break a humble man's sleep.

18:28 The more our hearts are fixed and enlarged in thanksgiving to God for our mercies the better disposed we shall be to bear with patience the afflictions mixed with them.

20:16–22 Though the man be the head, it does not therefore follow that he has the monopoly of the brains, and therefore he ought not, by any salique law, to have the monopoly of the crown. Many a masculine heart, and more than masculine, has been found in a female breast; nor is the treasure of wisdom the less valuable for being lodged in the weaker vessel.

21:22 Death is a Christian's last enemy, and a son of Anak; but, through him that triumphed for us, we hope to be more than conquerors at last, even over that enemy.

23:1 When we find death approaching we should endeavour both to honour God and to edify those about us with our last words. Let those that have had long experience of God's goodness and the pleasantness of wisdom, when they come to finish their course, leave a record of that experience and bear their testimony to the truth of the promise.

24:3 Many things, not in themselves sinful, turn into sin to us by our inordinately delighting in them.

1 Kings

2:28–34 Those who, by a lively faith, take hold on Christ and his righteousness with a resolution, if they perish, to perish there, shall find in him a more powerful protection than Joab found at the horns of the altar.

4:34 This puts an honour upon human learning, that Solomon was praised for it, and recommends it to the great men of the earth, as well worthy their diligent search.

7:21 Spiritual strength and stability are to be had at the door of God's temple, where we must wait for the gifts of grace in the use of the means of grace.

8:48 No place now, under the gospel, can be imagined to add any acceptableness to the prayers made in or towards it, as the temple then did. That was a shadow: the substance is Christ; whatever we ask in his name, it shall be given us.

9:27 Thus one nation needs another, Providence so ordering it that there may be mutual commerce and assistance; for not only as Christians, but as men, we are members one of another.

11:1 Many (says Bishop Hall) have had their head broken by their own rib.

12:10 That is not always the best sense that is best worded.

12:26–27 A practical disbelief of God's all-sufficiency is at the bottom of all our treacherous departures from him.

17:3 If Providence calls us to solitude and retirement, it becomes us to acquiesce; when we cannot be useful we must be patient, and when we cannot work for God we must sit still quietly for him.

19:19 We love God, and choose him, because he chose us, and loved us first.

20:31 See the uncertainty of human affairs; such turns are they subject to that the spoke which was uppermost may soon come to be undermost.

21:4 Discontent is a sin that is its own punishment and makes men torment themselves; it makes the spirit sad, the body sick, and all the enjoyments sour; it is the heaviness of the heart and the rottenness of the bones.

22:7 Whithersoever a good man goes he desires to take God along with him, and will acknowledge him in all his ways, ask leave of him, and look up to him for success. Whithersoever a good man goes he ought to take his religion along with him, and not be ashamed to own it, no, not when he is with those who have no kindness for it.

2 Kings to Job

2 Kings

1:3 It is a very wicked thing, upon any occasion or pretence whatsoever, to consult with the devil. This wickedness reigned in the heathen world (Isa. 47:12–13) and remains too much even in the Christian world, and the devil's kingdom is supported by it.

2:9 We all ought, both ministers and people, to set before us the example of our predecessors, to labour after their spirit, and to be earnest with God for that grace which carried them through their work and enabled them to finish well.

2:11 Thinking of divine things is good, but talking of them (if it come from the heart) is better, because for edification, 1 Cor. 14:4. Christ ascended as he was blessing his disciples.

2:13 There are remains of great and good men, which like this mantle, ought to be gathered up and preserved by the survivors, their sayings, their writings, their examples, that, as their works follow them in the reward of them, they may stay behind in the benefit of them.

4:26 When God calls away our dearest relations by death it becomes us quietly to say, 'It is well both with us and them'; it is well, for all is well that God does; all is well for those that are gone if they have gone to heaven, and all well with us that stay behind if by the affliction we are furthered in our way thither.

5:13 The methods prescribed for the healing of the leprosy of sin are so plain that we are utterly inexcusable if we do not observe them. It is but, 'Believe, and be saved'—'Repent, and be pardoned'—'Wash, and be clean.'

5:17 Perhaps the transport of his affection and veneration for the prophet … made him, as we say, love the very ground he went upon and desire to have some of it home with him. The modern compliment equivalent to this would be, 'Pray, sir, let me have your picture.'

9:22 What peace can sinners have with God, what peace with their own consciences, what good, what comfort, can they expect in life, in death, or after death, who go on still in their trespasses? No peace so long as sin is persisted in; but, as soon as it is repented of and forsaken, there is peace.

13:14 Elisha ... might be useful to the last, and yet not so famous as he had sometimes been. The time of his flourishing was less than the time of his living. Let not old people complain of obscurity, but rather be well pleased with retirement.

It may turn much to our spiritual advantage to attend the sick-beds and death-beds of good ministers and other good men, that we may learn to die, and may be encouraged in religion by the living comforts they have from it in a dying hour.

17:6 When we read of their [Israel's] entry under Hoshea the son of Nun who would have thought that such as this should be their exit under Hoshea son of Elah? Thus Rome's glory in Augustus sunk, many ages after, in Augustulus. Though we never read of those that were carried captive, nor have any reason to credit the conjecture of some (that they yet remain a distinct body in some remote corner of the world), yet a remnant of them did escape, to keep up the name of Israel, till it came to be worn by the gospel church, the spiritual Israel, in which it will ever remain, Gal. 6:16.

18:3 Let us not be frightened with an apprehension of the continual decay of virtue, as if, when times and men are bad, they must needs, of course, grow worse and worse; that does not follow, for, after many bad kings, God raised up one that was like David himself.

20:1 Neither greatness nor goodness can exempt us from sickness, from sore and mortal sicknesses. When we come to be sick … set the heart in order by renewed acts of repentance and faith, and resignation to God, with cheerful farewells to this world and welcomes to another; and, if not done before (which is the best and wisest course), set the house in order, make thy will, settle thy estate, put thy affairs in the best posture thou canst, for the ease of those that shall come after thee.

20:2 If the sentence was irreversible, yet prayer is one of the best preparations for death, because by it we fetch in strength and grace from God to enable us to finish well.

When we cannot be so private as we would in our devotions, nor perform them with the usual outward expressions of reverence and solemnity, yet we must not therefore omit them, but compose ourselves to them as well as we can.

20:3 The testimony of conscience for us that we have walked with God in our integrity will be much our support and rejoicing when we come to look death in the face, 2 Cor. 1:12.

It is in the nature of man to have some dread of the separation of soul and body, and it was not strange if the Old-Testament saints, to whom another world was but darkly revealed, were not so willing to leave this as Paul and other New-Testament saints were.

20:7 It is our duty, when we are sick, to make use of such means as are proper to help nature, else we do not trust God, but tempt him.

20:13 What is more commonly, and more innocently, done, than to show strangers the riches and rarities of a country—to show our friends our houses and their furniture, our gardens, stables and libraries? But if we do this in the pride of our hearts, as Hezekiah did, to gain applause from men, and not giving praise to God, it turns into sin to us, as it did to him.

22:2 The consideration of the time we unavoidably lost in our minority should quicken us, when we have come to years, to act with so much the more vigour in the service of God.

22:8 If the holy scriptures had not been of God, they would not have been in being at this day; God's care of the bible is a plain indication of his interest in it.

22:20 He died in the love and favour of God, which secure such a peace as no circumstances of dying, no, not dying in the field of war, could alter the nature of, or break in upon.

23:25 What great things we may bring to pass in the service of God if we be but lively and hearty in it!

23:29 God has promised to keep us *in all our ways*; but, if we go out of our way, we throw ourselves out of his protection.

25:9 It is observable that the second temple was burnt by the Romans the same month, and the same day of the month, that the first temple was burnt by the Chaldeans, which, Josephus says, was the tenth of August.

1 Chronicles

2:55 *Would to God that all the Lord's people were prophets*—all the families of Israel families of scribes, well instructed to the kingdom of heaven, and able to bring out of their treasury things new and old!

4:14 There was a valley where they lived which was, from them, called *the valley of craftsmen*. Those that are craftsmen are not therefore to be looked upon as mean men. These craftsmen, though two of a trade often disagree, yet chose to live together, for the improving of arts by comparing notes, and that they might support one another's reputation.

4:40 Those who dwell (as we do) in a fruitful country, and whose land is wide, and quiet, and peaceable, have reason to own themselves indebted to that God who *appoints the bounds of our habitation*.

5:1 Sin lessens men, thrusts them down from their excellency.

6:31 When the people of God come to the rest which remains for them above they shall take leave of all their burdens and be employed in everlasting songs.

7:24 A virtuous woman may be as great an honour and blessing to a family as a mighty man.

8:1–32 This holy man [Ezra] wrote as he was moved by the Holy Ghost; but there was no necessity for the making up of the defects, no, nor for the rectifying of the mistakes of these genealogies by inspiration. It was sufficient that he copied them out as they came to his hand, or so much of them as was requisite to the present purpose.

9:35–44 If we admit that there are in the originals, especially in these books, some errors of the transcribers, I should be tempted to think this repetition arose from a blunder. Some one, in copying out these genealogies, having written those words, v. 34 (*These dwelt at Jerusalem*), cast his eye on the same words, 8:28 (*these dwelt in Jerusalem*), and so went on with what followed there, instead of going on with what followed here; and when he perceived his mistake, was loth to make a blot in his book, and so let it stand. We have a rule in our law, *Redundans non nocet—Redundancies do no harm.*

21:13 Good men, even when God frowns upon them, think well of him.

24:5 The lot is an appeal to God, and ought to be managed with corresponding reverence and sincerity. I know not but it might still be used in faith in parallel cases, as an instituted ordinance.

2 Chronicles

8:5–6 Solomon ... spent his days ... not in his study, but in his country, in building cities and fortifying them, in a time of peace preparing for a time of war, which is as much a man's business as it is in summer to provide food for winter.

It is the interest of a state by all means possible to promote and encourage industry, and to keep its subjects from idleness.

16:1 How to reconcile the date of this event with the history of the kings I am quite at a loss. Baasha died in the twenty-sixth year of Asa, 1 Kings 16:8. How then could this be done in his thirty-sixth year, when Baasha's family was quite cut off, and Omri was upon the throne?

16:12 His [Asa's] making use of physicians was his duty; but trusting to them, and expecting from them which was to be had from God only, were his sin and folly. The help of creatures must always be used with an eye to the Creator, and in dependence upon him, who makes every creature that to us which it is, and without whom the most skilful and faithful are physicians of no value.

24:6 It is easier to build temples than to be temples to God. The repairing of churches is a good work, which all in their places should promote, for the decency and convenience of religious assemblies.

24:10 Many have honesty enough to follow that have not zeal enough to lead in that which is good. The throwing of money into a chest, through a hole in the lid of it, was a way that had not been used before, and perhaps the very novelty of the thing made it a successful expedient for the raising of money; a great deal was thrown in and with a great deal of cheerfulness: they all rejoiced, v. 10.

25:2 Such is the character of too many in this Laodicean age: they do that which is good, but not with the heart, not with a perfect heart.

25:9 What is it to trust in God, but to be willing to venture the loss of any thing for him, in confidence of the goodness of the security he gives us that we shall not lose by him, but that whatever we part with for his sake shall be made up to us in kind or kindness.

He [God] is just, and he is good, and he is solvent.

26:19 If presumptuous men will not be made to see their error by the judgments of God's mouth, they shall be made to see it by the judgments of his hand.

29:30 It is not enough for us to be where God is worshipped, if we do not ourselves worship him, and that not with bodily exercise only, which profits little, but with the heart.

30:19 The great thing required in our attendance upon God in solemn ordinances is that we *prepare our hearts to seek him*, that we be sincere and upright in all we do, that the inward man be engaged and employed in it, and that we make heart-work of it; it is all nothing without this.

31:13 That will be given cheerfully by the public which appears to be well husbanded. Church treasures are not to be hoarded any longer than till there is occasion for them, lest even the rust should be a witness against those who hoard them.

31:18 In maintaining ministers, regard must be had to their families, that not they only, but theirs, may have food convenient. In some countries where ministers have their salary paid them by the state an addition is made to it upon the birth of a child.

31:21 What is undertaken with a sincere regard to the glory of God, will succeed to our own honour and comfort at last.

33:13 Afflictions are continued no longer than till they have done their work.

Ezra

8:17 The furnishing of God's house with good ministers is a good work, which will redound to the comfort and credit of all that have a hand in it.

10:2 Such marriages (with unbelievers), it is certain, are sinful, and ought not to be made, but they are not null. That which ought not to have been done must, when done, abide. Our rule, under the gospel, is, *If a brother has a wife that believeth not*, and, *she be pleased to dwell with him, let him not put her away*, 1 Cor. 7:12–13.

10:14 Thus *take time and we shall have done the sooner;* whereas, if we do it in a hurry, we shall do it by halves, v. 14.

Nehemiah

1:4 Let those who are forming any good designs for the service of the public take God along with them for the first conception of them, and utter all their projects before him; this is the way to prosper in them.

5:3 If men borrow large sums to trade with, to increase their stocks, or to purchase land, there is no reason why the lender should not share with the borrower in his profit; or if to spend upon their lusts, or repair what they have so spent, why should they not pay for their extravagancies? But if the poor borrow to maintain their families, and we be able to help them, it is certain we ought either to lend freely what they have occasion for, or (if they be not likely to repay it), to give freely something towards it.

7:64 Blessed be God that our faith and hope are not built on the niceties of names and numbers, genealogy and chronology, but on the great things of the law and gospel.

8:1–3 Masters of families should bring their families with them to the public worship of God. Women and children have souls to save, and are therefore concerned to acquaint themselves with the word of God and attend on the means of knowledge and grace. Little ones, as they come to the exercise of reason, must be trained up in the exercises of religion. And, upon special occasions, we must be willing to attend for many hours together on the reading and expounding of the word of God: those mentioned here were thus employed for six hours.

8:7–8 Reading is good, and preaching is good, but expounding brings the reading and the preaching together, and thus makes the reading the more intelligible and the preaching the more convincing.

8:10 Holy joy will be oil to the wheels of our obedience.

10:31 Those that covenant to keep all God's commandments must particularly covenant to keep sabbaths well; for the profanation of them is an inlet to other instances of profaneness. The sabbath is a market day for our souls, but not for our bodies.

10:32 It is likely to go well with our houses when care is taken that the work of God's house go on well. The work of the house of God is likely to go on when those that serve at the altar live, and live comfortably upon the altar.

10:37–39 Though they paid great taxes to the kings of Persia, and had much hardship put upon them, they would not make that an excuse for not paying their tithes. We must do what we can in works of piety and charity notwithstanding the taxes we pay to the government.

12:36–40 The crowd of people, it is likely, walked on the ground, some within the wall and others without, one end of this ceremony being to affect them with the mercy they were giving thanks for, and to perpetuate the remembrance of it among them. Processions, for such purposes, have their use.

12:44–45 When the joy of the Lord thus engages us to our duty, and enlarges us in it, it is then an earnest of that joy which, in concurrence with the perfection of holiness, will be our everlasting bliss.

The surest way for ministers to recommend themselves to their people, and gain an interest in their affections, is *to wait on their ministry* (Rom. 12:7), to be humble and industrious, and to mind their business. When these did so the people thought nothing too much to do for them, to encourage them.

Esther

1:12 When wives *despise their husbands*, whom they ought to *reverence* (Eph. 5:33), and contend for *dominion* over those to whom they ought to be in *subjection* (1 Peter 3:1), there cannot but be continual guilt and grief, confusion and every evil work.

2:20 All truths are not to be spoken at all times, though an untruth is not to be spoken at any time.

3:15 It is an absurd and impious thing to indulge ourselves in mirth and pleasure when the church is in distress and the public are perplexed.

4:14 There is a wise counsel and design in all the providences of God, which is unknown to us till it is accomplished, but it will prove, in the issue, that they are all intended for, and centre in, the good of the church.

We should every one of us consider for what end God has put us in the place where we are, and study to answer that end; and, when any particular opportunity of serving God and our generation offers itself, we must take care that we do not let it slip; for we are entrusted with it that we might improve it.

5:8 What is hastily asked is often as hastily denied; but what is asked with a pause deserves to be considered.

10:3 Thanks be to God, such a government as this we are blessed with, which *seeks the welfare of our people, speaking peace to all their seed*. God continue it long, very long, and grant us, under the happy protection and influence of it, to *live quiet and peaceable lives, in godliness, honesty* and charity!

Job

1:4 Good parents desire, promote, and rejoice in, their children's wealth and prosperity as their own. Young people may be allowed a youthful liberty, provided they flee youthful lusts.

2:13 Coming to comfort him ... they resolved to stay with him till they saw him mend or end, and therefore took lodgings near him.

5:24 Family piety crowns family peace and prosperity. The greatest blessing, both in our employments and in our enjoyments, is to be kept from sin in them.

5:25 Children ... if they are truly good, they are truly great, how small a figure soever they may make in the world.

5:26 Our times are in God's hand; it is well they are so, for he will take care that those who are his shall die in the best time: however their death may seem to us untimely, it will be found not unseasonable.

6:9 How uneasy soever the soul's confinement in the body may be, it must by no means break prison, but wait for a fair discharge.

6:15 We cannot expect too little from the creature nor too much from the Creator.

7:3 When we are disabled to work for God, if we will but sit still quietly for him, it is all one; we shall be accepted.

7:14 We have reason to pray to God that our dreams may neither defile nor disquiet us, neither tempt us to sin nor torment us with fear, that he who keeps Israel, and neither slumbers nor sleeps, may keep us when we slumber and sleep, that the devil may not then do us a mischief, either as an insinuating serpent or as a roaring lion, and to bless God if we lie down and our sleep is sweet and we are not thus scared.

8:4 Extraordinary afflictions are not always the punishment of extraordinary sins, but sometimes the trial of extraordinary graces.

9:8 As long as he pleases he preserves the settled course and order of nature; and this is a continued creation.

9:9 The stars of which these [constellations] are composed he made at first, and put into that order, and he still makes them, preserves them in being, and guides their motions.

9:25–26 What little need have we of pastimes, and what great need to redeem time, when time runs out, runs on so fast towards eternity, which comes as time goes!

10:8 The soul is the life, the soul is the man, and this is the gift of God: *Thou hast granted me life*, breathed into me the breath of life, without which the body would be but a worthless carcase.

10:14 So hard is it to see love in God's heart when we see frowns in his face and a rod in his hand.

11:9 The eye can see the ocean but not see over it.

12:17–19 Witness the glorious Revolution (1688–1689) in our own land twenty years ago, in which we saw as happy an exposition as ever was given of this discourse of Job's.

12:25 God can soon nonplus the deepest politicians and bring the greatest wits to their wit's end, to show that wherein they deal proudly he is above them.

13:15 We must rejoice in God when we have nothing else to rejoice in, and cleave to him, yea, though we cannot for the present find comfort in him. In a dying hour we must derive from him living comforts; and this is to trust in him though he slay us.

14:22 Dying work is hard work; dying pangs are, commonly, sore pangs. It is folly therefore for men to defer their repentance to a death-bed, and to have that to do which is the one thing needful when they are really unfit to do any thing: but it is true wisdom, by making our peace with God in Christ and keeping a good conscience, to treasure up comforts which will support and relieve us against the pains and sorrows of a dying hour.

15:16 It is natural to sinners to commit iniquity. It gratifies, but does not satisfy, the appetites of the old man.

18:4 Anger is a sin that is its own punishment.

19:25 Our heavenly inheritance was mortgaged by sin; we are ourselves utterly unable to redeem it; Christ is near of kin to us, the next kinsman that is able to redeem; he has paid our debt, satisfied God's justice for sin, and so has taken off the mortgage and made a new settlement of the inheritance.

Our persons also want a Redeemer; we are sold for sin, and sold under sin; our Lord Jesus has wrought out a redemption for us, and proclaims redemption to us, and so he is truly the Redeemer. He knows enough, and knows to good purpose, who knows Christ to be his Redeemer.

19:26 He shall stand, at the last, on the dust to which this earth will be reduced by the conflagration. The same power that made man's body at first, out of common dust, can raise it out of its own dust. The separate soul has eyes wherewith to see God, eyes of the mind; but Job speaks of seeing him with eyes of flesh; the same body that died shall rise again, a true body, but a glorious body, fit for the employments and entertainments of that world, and therefore a *spiritual body*, 1 Cor. 15:44.

19:28 In our conduct towards our brethren ... we are to believe that many have the root of the matter in them who are not in everything of our mind—who have their follies, and weaknesses, and mistakes—and to conclude that it is at our peril if we persecute any such. Woe be to him that offends one of those little ones! God will resent and revenge it.

21:11 Dancing is fittest for children, who know not better how to spend their time and whose innocency guards them against the mischiefs that commonly attend it.

21:21–26 There is one way into the world, we say, but many out; yet, as some are born by quick and easy labour, others by that which is hard and lingering, so dying is to some much more terrible than to others; and, since the death of the body is the birth of the soul into another world, death-bed agonies may not unfitly be compared to child-bed throes.

22:24–25 Worldlings make gold their God, saints make God their gold; and those that are enriched with his favour and grace may truly be said *to have abundance of the best gold*, and best laid up.

23:10 Those that go gold into the furnace will come out no worse.

23:13 Prayer has prevailed to change God's way and his providence, but never was his will or purpose changed.

23:17 This may help to reconcile us to death, whenever it comes, that we do not know what evil we may be taken away from. Remember that to the upright there sometimes arises a marvellous light in the darkness; however, there is reserved for them a more marvellous light after it.

25:5 The heavenly bodies are often clouded; we plainly see spots in the moon, and, with the help of glasses, may sometimes discern spots upon the sun too: but God sees spots in them that we do not see.

26:11–14 When we have said all we can, concerning God, we must even do as St Paul does (Rom. 11:33); despairing to find the bottom, we must sit down at the brink, and adore the depth: *O the depth of the wisdom and knowledge of God!*

26:13 If the visible heavens be so glorious, what are those that are out of sight! From the beauteous garniture of the ante-chamber we may infer the precious furniture of the presence-chamber.

27:16–17 Money is like manure, good for nothing if it be not spread.

27:20–21 Death, to a godly man, is like a fair gale of wind to convey him to the heavenly country, but, to a wicked man, it is like an east wind, a storm, a tempest, that hurries him away in confusion and amazement, to destruction.

28:12 Such is the degeneracy of human nature that there is no true wisdom to be found with any but those who are born again, and who, through grace, partake of the divine nature.

28:15 It is *better to get wisdom than gold*. Gold is another's, wisdom our own; gold is for the body and time, wisdom for the soul and eternity. Let that which is most precious in God's account be so in ours.

34:14–15 God ... can soon bring us to dust; there needs not any positive act of his omnipotence to do it; if he do but withdraw that concurrence of his providence by which we live, *if he gather unto himself that spirit and breath* which was from his hand at first and is still in his hand, we expire immediately, like an animal in an air-pump when the air is exhausted.

35:9–10 Of the many that are afflicted and oppressed, few get the good they might get by their affliction. It should drive them to God, but how seldom is this the case!

35:10 Something like logic, and philosophy, and politics, has been observed among the brute creatures, but never any thing of divinity or religion.

35:12 If we cry to God for the removal of the oppression and affliction we are under, and it is not removed, the reason is not because the Lord's hand is shortened or his ear heavy, but because the affliction has not done its work.

36:12 As what goes up a vapour comes down a shower, so what goes up sin, if not repented of, will come down wrath.

36:24 Look at the minutest works of nature through a microscope; do they not appear curious? The eternal power and godhead of the Creator are *clearly seen and understood* by the *things that are made*, Rom. 1:20.

37:14–18 The gravitation of bodies, and the cohesion of the parts of matter, are most certain, and yet unaccountable. If we foresee the change of weather a few hours before, by vulgar observation, or when second causes have begun to work by the weather-glass, yet how little do these show us of the purposes of God by these changes!

38:31 God has the stars of heaven under his command and cognizance, but we have them not under ours. Our meditations are now to rise higher, far above the clouds, to the glorious lights above. God mentions particularly, not the planets, which move in lower orbs, but the fixed stars, which are much higher. It is supposed that they have an influence upon this earth, notwithstanding their vast distance, not upon the minds of men or the events of providence (men's fate is not determined by their stars), but upon the ordinary course of nature; they are set for signs and seasons, for days and years, Gen. 1:14.

40:19 Those that will peruse the accounts given by historians of the elephant will find that his capacities approach nearer to those of reason than the capacities of any other brute-creature whatsoever, and therefore he is fitly called *the chief of the ways of God*, in the inferior part of the creation, no creature below man being preferable to him.

42:10 God is better served and pleased with our warm devotions than with our warm disputations.

Psalms to Song of Solomon

Psalms

1:1 The Lord knows those that are his by name, but we must know them by their character.

1:2 All that are well pleased that there is a God must be well pleased that there is a Bible, a revelation of God, of his will, and of the only way to happiness in him.

2:6 The evangelical law of Christ is said to *go forth from Zion* (Isa. 2:3; Micah 4:2), and therefore that is spoken of as the head-quarters of this general, the royal seat of this prince, in whom the children of men shall be joyful.

3:1–3 Perils and frights should drive us to God, not drive us from him.

3:3 If, in the worst of times, God's people can lift up their heads with joy, knowing that all shall work for good to them, they will own that it is God that is the lifter up of their head, that gives them both cause to rejoice and hearts to rejoice.

4:1 The New Testament appoints all Christians to sing (Eph. 5:19; Col. 3:16), from whom it is expected that they do it decently, not artfully; and therefore there is not now so much occasion for musical instruments as there was then: the melody is to be made in the heart.

4:4, 8 When you awake in the night meditate upon God, and the things that belong to your peace. So a good man, having by faith and prayer cast his care upon God, sleeps and rests night and day, and is very easy, leaving it to his God to perform all things for him and prepared to welcome his holy will.

5:3 Morning prayer is our duty; we are fittest for prayer when we are in the most fresh, and lively, and composed frame, got clear of the slumbers of the night, revived by them, and not yet filled with the business of the day.

7:1 The injuries men do us should drive us to God, for to him we may commit our cause.

7:11 As his mercies are new every morning towards his people, so his anger is new every morning against the wicked, upon the fresh occasions given for it by their renewed transgressions.

8:3 It is our duty to consider the heavens. We see them, we cannot but see them. By this, among other things, man is distinguished from the beasts, that, while *they* are so framed as to look downwards to the earth, man is made erect to look upwards towards heaven.

9:17 Forgetfulness of God is the cause of all the wickedness of the wicked.

11:4 *His eyes behold, his eyelids try, the children of men;* he not only sees them, but he sees through them.

12:2 This is the devil's image complete, a complication of malice and falsehood.

12:6 Though men are false, God is faithful; though they are not to be trusted, God is.

13:1–4 We should never allow ourselves to make any complaints but what are fit to be offered up to God and what drive us to our knees.

14:1 Atheistical thoughts are very foolish wicked thoughts, and they are at the bottom of a great deal of the wickedness that is in the world. No man will say, *There is no God* till he is so hardened in sin that it has become his interest that there should be none to call him to an account.

16:3 There are saints in the earth; and saints on earth we must all be, or we shall never be saints in heaven.

16:6 Gracious persons, though they still covet more of God, never covet more than God.

17:5 Those that are, through grace, going in God's paths, have need to pray, and do pray, that their goings may be held up in those paths; for we stand no longer than he is pleased to hold us, we go no further than he is pleased to lead us, bear us up, and carry us.

17:15 We must entertain ourselves from day to day with the contemplation of the beauty of the Lord; and, when we awake every morning, we must be satisfied with his likeness set before us in his word, and with his likeness stamped upon us by his renewing grace. Our experience of God's favour to us, and our conformity to him, should yield us more satisfaction than those have whose belly is filled with the delights of sense.

18:16 David was found a praying man, and God was found a prayer-hearing God. If we pray as he did, we shall speed as he did. Though distress drive us to prayer, God will not therefore be deaf to us; nay, being a God of pity, he will be the more ready to succour us.

18:18 God will not only deliver his people out of their troubles in due time, but he will sustain them and bear them up under their troubles in the mean time.

19:1 They [the heavens] plainly speak themselves to be God's handy-works; for they could not exist from eternity; all succession and motion must have had a beginning; they could not make themselves, that is a contradiction; they could not be produced by a casual hit of atoms, that is an absurdity, fit rather to be bantered than reasoned with: therefore they must have a Creator, who can be no other than an eternal mind, infinitely wise, powerful and good.

19:7 The holy scripture, as it is a rule both of our duty to God and of our expectation from him, is of much greater use and benefit to us than day or night, than the air we breathe in, or the light of the sun.

19:10 Gold is of the earth, earthly; but grace is the image of the heavenly. Gold is only for the body and the concerns of time; but grace is for the soul and the concerns of eternity.

20:3 By this we may now know that God accepts our spiritual sacrifices, if by his Spirit he kindles in our souls a holy fire of pious and divine affection and with that makes our hearts burn within us.

21:8 There is no escaping God's avenging eye, no going out of the reach of his hand; rocks and mountains will be no better shelter at last than fig-leaves were at first.

22:1 When we want the faith of assurance we must live by a faith of adherence.

22:23 The business of Christians, particularly in their solemn religious assemblies, is to praise and glorify God with a holy awe and reverence of his majesty, and therefore those that are here called upon to praise God are called upon to fear him.

22:27 Serious reflection is the first step, and a good step it is, towards true conversion. We must consider and turn. The prodigal came first to himself, and then to his father.

23:6 If God's goodness to us be like the morning light, which shines more and more to the perfect day, let not ours to him be like the morning cloud and the early dew that passeth away.

25:7 When God pardons sin he is said to *remember it no more*, which denotes a plenary remission; he forgives and forgets.

25:8 The devil leads men blindfold to hell, but God enlightens men's eyes, sets things before them in a true light, and so leads them to heaven. If we choose the right way, he that directed our choice will direct our steps, and will lead us in it. If we choose wisely, God will give us grace to walk wisely.

25:18 When at any time we are in trouble we should be more

concerned about our sins, to get them pardoned, than about our afflictions, to get them removed.

26:12 Those that hate the congregation of evil-doers shall be joined to the congregation of the righteous and join with them in praising God; and it is pleasant doing that in good company; the more the better: it is the more like heaven.

27:8 God calls us to seek his face in our conversion to him and in our converse with him.

29:2 If we would, in hearing and praying, and other acts of devotion, receive grace from God, we must make it our business to give glory to God.

30:Title The houses we dwell in should, at our first entrance upon them, be dedicated to God, as little sanctuaries. We must solemnly commit ourselves, our families, and all our family affairs, to God's guidance and care, must pray for his presence and blessing, must devote ourselves and all ours to his glory, and must resolve both that we will put away iniquity far from our tabernacles and that we and our houses will serve the Lord both in the duties of family worship and in all instances of gospel obedience.

31:22 It is a common thing to speak amiss when we speak in haste and without consideration; but what we speak amiss in haste we must repent of at leisure, particularly that which we have spoken distrustfully of God.

32:1–2 When sin is pardoned, it is covered with the robe of Christ's righteousness ... they [our sins] are not covered from us (no; *My sin is ever before me*) nor covered from God's omniscience, but from his vindictive justice.

32:5 God is more ready to pardon sin, upon our repentance, than we are to repent in order to the obtaining of pardon.

33:3 Here is a good rule for this duty [of singing with a harp]: 'Do it *skilfully*, and *with a loud noise*; let it have the best both of head and heart; let it be done intelligently and with a clear head, affectionately and with a warm heart.'

33:15 The artist that made the clock can account for the motions of every wheel.

33:20 We must wait for God. We must attend the motions of his providence, and accommodate ourselves to them, and patiently expect the issue of them.

34:3 We cannot make God greater or higher than he is; but if we adore him as infinitely great, and higher than the highest, he is pleased to reckon this magnifying and exalting him.

34:5 When we look to the world we are darkened, we are perplexed, and at a loss; but when we look to God, from him we have the light both of direction and joy, and our way is made both plain and pleasant.

34:7 God makes use of the attendance of the good spirits for the protection of his people from the malice and power of evil spirits; and the holy angels do us more good offices every day than we are aware of.

34:17 It is the constant practice of good people, when they are in distress, to cry unto God, and it is their constant comfort that God hears them.

36:8 The pleasures of sense are putrid puddle-water; those of faith are pure and pleasant, *clear as crystal*, Rev. 22:1.

37:6 If we take care to keep a good conscience, we may leave it to God to take care of our good name.

38:5 A slight sore, neglected, may prove of fatal consequence, and so may a slight sin slighted and left unrepented of.

38:17 Good men, by setting their sorrow continually before them, have been ready to halt, who, by setting God always before them, have kept their standing.

39:4 What death is: ... To the wicked man it is the end of all joys; to a godly man it is the end of all griefs.

39:6 Man takes a great deal of pains to *heap up riches*, and they are but like heaps of manure in the furrows of the field, good for nothing unless they be spread.

40:2 Christ is the rock on which a poor soul may stand fast, and on whose mediation alone between us and God we can build any solid hopes or satisfaction.

40:8 When the law of God is written in our hearts our duty will be our delight.

42:1 Sometimes God teaches us effectually to know the worth of mercies by the want of them, and whets our appetite for the means of grace by cutting us short in those means.

Lamenting after God is as sure an evidence that we love him as rejoicing in God.

42:6 When we cannot get relief for our burdened spirits by pleading with ourselves, we should try what we can do by praying to God and leaving our case with him. We cannot still these winds and waves; but we know who can.

43:3 Those whom God leads he leads to his holy hill, and to his tabernacles; those therefore who pretend to be led by the Spirit, and yet turn their backs upon instituted ordinances, certainly deceive themselves.

44:9 God's people, when they are cast down, are tempted to think themselves cast off and forsaken of God; but it is a mistake. *Hath God cast away his people? God forbid*, Rom. 11:1.

45:2 The beauties of the Lord Jesus, as God, as Mediator, far surpass those of human nature in general and those which the most amiable and excellent of the children of men are endowed with; there is more in Christ to engage our love than there is or can be in any creature.

46:2 The church shall survive the world, and be in bliss when that is in ruins. It is *built upon a rock*, and the *gates of hell shall not prevail against it*.

46:8 War is a tragedy which commonly destroys the stage it is acted on; David carried the war into the enemies' country; and O what desolations did it make there!

47:1 Such expressions of pious and devout affections as to some may seem indecent and imprudent ought not to be hastily censured and condemned, much less ridiculed, because, if they come from an upright heart, God will accept the strength of this affection and excuse the weakness of the expressions of it.

48:14 If we take the Lord for our God, he will conduct and convey us safely to death, through death, and beyond death—down to death and up again to glory.

49:2 Poor people are as much in danger from an inordinate desire towards the wealth of the world as rich people from an inordinate delight in it.

49:7–8 Everlasting life is a jewel of too great a value to be purchased by the wealth of this world.

49:14 The beauty of holiness is that which the grave, that consumes all other beauty, cannot touch, or do any damage to.

50:14 Dr Hammond applies this to the great gospel ordinance of the eucharist, in which … instead of all the Old Testament types of a Christ to come, we have that blessed memorial of a Christ already come.

50:22 Forgetfulness of God is at the bottom of all the wickedness of the wicked.

50:23 Thanksgiving is good, but thanks-living is better.

51:5 We have from our birth the snares of sin in our bodies, the seeds of sin in our souls, and a stain of sin upon both.

55:6 Gracious souls wish to retire from the hurry and bustle of this world, that they may sweetly enjoy God and themselves; and, if there be any true peace on this side heaven, it is they that enjoy it in those retirements.

56:3 There are some times which are, in a special manner, times of fear with God's people; in these times it is their duty and interest to trust in God as their God, and to know whom they have trusted. This will fix the heart and keep it in peace.

As we must not trust to an arm of flesh when it is engaged for us, so we must not be afraid of an arm of flesh when it is stretched out against us.

56:8 What was sown a tear, will come up a pearl.

59:13 The design of God's judgments is to convince men that the Lord reigns, that he fulfils his own counsels, gives law to all the creatures, and disposes all things to his own glory, so that the greatest of men are under his check, and he makes what use he pleases of them.

59:16–17 God brings his people into trouble, that they may experience his power and mercy in protecting and sheltering them, and may have occasion to praise him.

61:2 That which separates us from our other comforts should drive us so much the nearer to God, the fountain of all comfort.

63:2 The more faith is acted the more active it is.

Gracious souls look down upon the world with a holy disdain and look up to God with a holy desire. When we are deprived of the benefit of public ordinances we should desire and endeavour to keep up the same communion with God in our retirements that we have had in the great congregation. A closet may be turned into a little sanctuary. When we are alone we may have the Father with us, and that is enough.

63:3 We must praise God with joyful lips; we must address ourselves to that and other duties of religion with great cheerfulness, and speak forth the praises of God from a principle of holy joy. Praising lips must be joyful lips.

63:6 Thoughts of God must not be transient thoughts, passing through the mind, but abiding thoughts, dwelling in the mind.

66:16 We should take all occasions to tell one another of the great and kind things which God has done for us, especially which he has done for our souls, the spiritual blessings with which he has blessed us in heavenly things; these we should be most affected with ourselves, and therefore with these we should be desirous to affect others.

66:19–20 What we win by prayer we must wear with praise.

67:5 A face of religion appears upon a land when God is publicly owned and the ordinances of religious worship are duly celebrated in religious assemblies.

67:7 When the gospel begins to spread it shall get ground more and more, till it reach the ends of the earth.

68:35 Out of heaven, his holy place above, he does, and will, show himself a terrible God. Nor is any attribute of God more dreadful to sinners than his holiness.

70:4 A heart to love the salvation of the Lord, and to prefer it before any secular advantages whatsoever, so as cheerfully to quit all rather than hazard our salvation, is a good evidence of our interest in it and title to it.

71:6 He that was our help from our birth ought to be our hope from our youth.

71:23–24 My lips shall rejoice, but that is nothing; lip-labour, though ever so well laboured, if that be all, is but lost labour in serving God; the soul must be at work, and with all that is within us we must bless his holy name, else all about us is worth little.

72:1 Those have little love either to God or man, and are of a very narrow selfish spirit, who care not what becomes of the world and the church when they are gone.

73:6 It is no harm to wear a chain or necklace; but when pride ties it on, when it is worn to gratify a vain mind, it ceases to be an ornament. It is not so much what the dress or apparel is (though we have rules for that, 1 Tim. 2:9) as what principle ties it on and with what spirit it is worn.

73:7 See what the excess of pleasure is; the moderate use of it enlightens the eyes, but those that indulge themselves inordinately in the delights of sense have their eyes ready to start out of their heads.

73:15 It is bad to think ill, but it is worse to speak it.

We must think twice before we speak once, both because some things may be thought which yet may not be spoken and because the second thoughts may correct the mistakes of the first.

73:25 Our desires must not only be offered up to God, but they must all terminate in him, desiring nothing more than God, but still more and more of him.

75:1 There are many works which God does for his people that may truly be called *wondrous works*, out of the common course of providence and quite beyond our expectation.

77:2 Days of trouble must be days of prayer, days of inward trouble especially, when God seems to have withdrawn from us; we must seek him and seek till we find him.

Those that are under trouble of mind must not think to drink it away, or laugh it away, but must pray it away.

78:4 That which we are to transmit to our children is not only the knowledge of languages, arts and sciences, liberty and property, but especially the praises of the Lord, and his strength appearing in the wonderful works he has done. Our great care must be to lodge our religion, that great deposit, pure and entire in the hands of those that succeed us.

78:8 Hypocrisy is the high road to apostasy.

78:9 Weapons of war stand men in little stead without a martial spirit, and that is gone if God be gone.

78:21–22 Those cannot be said to trust in God's salvation as their felicity at last who cannot find in their hearts to trust in his providence for food convenient in the way to it.

79:9 We should be more earnest with God in prayer for the removal of our sins than for the removal of our afflictions, and the pardon of them is the foundation and sweetness of our deliverance.

81:2–3 The pleasantness of the harp and the awfulness of the trumpet intimate to us that God is to be worshipped with cheerfulness and holy joy, with reverence and godly fear.

81:11 All the wickedness of the wicked world is owing to the wilfulness of the wicked will.

84:1 How lovely is the sanctuary in the eyes of all that are truly sanctified!

84:5 Those are truly happy who go forth, and go on, in the exercises of religion, not in their own strength (for then the work is sure to miscarry), but in the strength of the grace of Jesus Christ, from whom all our sufficiency is.

Those who have the new Jerusalem in their eye must have the ways that lead to it in their heart

84:10–12 If we cannot go to the house of the Lord, we may go by faith to the Lord of the house, and in him we shall be happy and may be easy.

85:4 All those whom God will save sooner or later he will turn. If no conversion, no salvation.

85:10 Our salvation is so well contrived, so well concerted, that God may have mercy upon poor sinners, and be at peace with them, without any wrong to his truth and righteousness.

85:12 All good comes from God's goodness; and when mercy, truth, and righteousness, have a sovereign influence on men's hearts and lives, all good may be expected.

86:1 The flourishes of wit are not the proper ornaments of prayer.

86:4 Prayer is the nurse of spiritual joy.

88:18 Next to the comforts of religion are those of friendship and society; therefore to be friendless is (as to this life) almost to be comfortless; and to those who have had friends, but have lost them, the calamity is the more grievous.

89:47 Those whose days are few and full of trouble may yet glorify God and do some good, may keep their communion with God and get to heaven, and then they are not made in vain.

90:12 It is an excellent art rightly *to number our days*, so as not to be out in our calculation, as he was who counted upon many years to come when, that night, his soul was required of him.

91:5 Whatever is done, our heavenly Father's will is done; and we have no reason to be afraid of that.

92:1 The sabbath day must be a day, not only of holy rest, but of holy work, and the rest is in order to the work. The proper work of the sabbath is praising God; every sabbath day must be a thanksgiving day; and the other services of the day must be in order to this, and therefore must by no means thrust this into a corner.

92:14 The last days of the saints are sometimes their best days, and their last work is their best work. This indeed shows that they are upright; perseverance is the surest evidence of sincerity.

94:12 When we are chastened we must pray to be taught, and look into the law as the best expositor of Providence. It is not the chastening itself that does good, but the teaching that goes along with it and is the exposition of it.

95:7–8 Nothing is more offensive to God than disbelief of his promise and despair of the performance of it because of some difficulties that seem to lie in the way.

95:10 Sins are errors, practical errors, errors in heart; such there are, and as fatal as errors in the head.

101:2 It is a desirable thing, when a man has a house of his own, to have God come to him and dwell with him in it; and those may expect God's presence that walk with *a perfect heart* in *a perfect way*.

102:28 Since Christ is the same, the church shall continue from one generation to another; from the eternity of the head we may infer the perpetuity of the body, though often weak and distempered, and even at death's door.

103:7 Divine revelation is one of the first and greatest of divine favours with which the church is blessed; for God restores us to himself by revealing himself to us, and gives us all good by giving us knowledge.

104:1 When we are addressing ourselves to any religious service we must *stir up ourselves to take hold on God* in it (Isa. 64:7); so David does here. 'Come, my soul, where art thou? What art thou thinking of? Here is work to be done, good work, angels' work; set about it in good earnest; let all the powers and faculties be engaged and employed in it: *Bless the Lord, O my soul!*'

104:24 The works of art, the more closely they are looked upon with the help of microscopes, the more rough they appear; the works of nature through these glasses appear more fine and exact. They are all made in wisdom, for they are all made to answer the end they were designed to serve, the good of the universe, in order to the glory of the universal Monarch.

104:35 This is the first time that we meet with *Hallelujah*; and it comes in here upon occasion of the destruction of the wicked; and the last time that we meet with it is upon a similar occasion. When the New-Testament Babylon is consumed, this is the burden of the song, *Hallelujah*, Rev. 19:1, 3, 4, 6. [Note: 'Praise ye the Lord' is 'Hallelujah' in Hebrew.]

107:24–28 The deep itself is a wonder, its vastness, its saltness, its ebbing and flowing. The great variety of living creatures in the sea is wonderful. Let those that go to sea be led, by all the wonders they observe there, to consider and adore the infinite perfections of that God whose the sea is, for he made it and manages it.

107:27 Those that have the Lord for their God have a present and powerful help in that and every other time of need, so that when they are at their wit's end they are not at their faith's end.

111:1 The title of the psalm being *Hallelujah*, the psalmist (as every author ought to have) has an eye to his title, and keeps to his text. [Note: 'Praise ye the Lord' is 'Hallelujah' in Hebrew.]

111:10 A great understanding those have that know God's commandments and can discourse learnedly of them, but a good understanding have those that do them and walk according to them.

113:6 If it be such condescension for God to behold things in heaven and earth, what an amazing condescension was it for the Son of God to come from heaven to earth and take our nature upon him, that he might *seek and save those that were lost*! Herein indeed he humbled himself.

116:6 God's people are never brought so low but that everlasting arms are under them, and those cannot sink who are thus sustained.

117:2 God's mercy is the fountain of all our comforts and his truth the foundation of all our hopes, and therefore for both we must praise the Lord.

119:7 God's judgments are all righteous, and therefore it is desirable not only to learn them, but to be learned in them, *mighty in the scriptures*.

As long as we live we must be scholars in Christ's school, and sit at his feet; but we should aim to be head-scholars, and to get into the highest form.

119:17 Life is ... a choice mercy, because it is an opportunity of obeying God in this world, where there are so few that do glorify him.

119:32 The joy of our Lord should be wheels to our obedience.

119:35 Both the good head and the good heart are from the good grace of God, and both are necessary to every good work.

119:36 Those ... that would have the love of God rooted in them must get the love of the world rooted out of them; for *the friendship of the world is enmity with God*.

119:45 Licentiousness is bondage to the greatest of tyrants; conscientiousness is freedom to the meanest of prisoners, John 8:32, 36; Luke 1:74–75.

119:59 Penitent reflections must produce pious resolutions.

119:62 Public worship will not excuse us from secret worship.

119:71 It has been the advantage of God's people to be afflicted.

119:75 Afflictions are in the covenant, and therefore they are not only not meant for our hurt, but they are really intended for our good.

119:86 True religion, if it be worth any thing, is worth every thing, and therefore worth suffering for.

119:93 If we are quickened by the word, we shall never forget it; nay, that word that does really quicken us to and in our duty is not forgotten; though the expressions be lost, if the impressions remain, it is well.

119:98 A good man, wherever he goes, carries his Bible along with him, if not in his hands, yet in his head and in his heart.

119:112 Those that would have the blessings of God's testimonies must come under the bonds of his statutes.

119:116–117 We stand no longer than God holds us and go no further than he carries us.

119:136 The sins of sinners are the sorrows of saints. We must mourn for that which we cannot mend.

119:162 The more reverence we have for the word of God, the more joy we shall find in it.

119:163 Love and hatred are the leading affections of the soul; if those be fixed aright, the rest move accordingly.

125:4 Those that are as they should be shall be as they would be, provided they be *upright in heart*, that they be really as good as they seem to be.

131:2 When our condition is not to our mind we must bring our mind to our condition; and then we are easy to ourselves and all about us.

132:3–5 When needful work is to be done for God it is good for us to task ourselves, and tie ourselves to a time, because we are apt to put off. It is good in the morning to cut out work for the day, binding ourselves that we will do it before we sleep, only with submission to Providence; for we *know not what a day may bring forth*.

134:3 We must pray for those that exhort us. Though *the less is blessed of the greater* (Heb. 7:7), yet the greater must be prayed for by the less.

135:7 All the powers of nature prove the greatness of the God of nature, from whom they are derived and on whom they depend.

138:2 The wonders of grace exceed the wonders of nature; and what is discovered of God by revelation is much greater than what is discovered by reason.

140:5 Great persecutors have often been great politicians, which has indeed made them the more formidable; but *the Lord preserves the simple* without all those arts.

141:1 Those that cry in prayer may hope to be heard in prayer, not for their loudness, but their liveliness. He that believes does not make haste, but he that prays may be earnest with God to make haste.

141:6 When the world is bitter the word is sweet.

142:4 How many good men have been deceived by such swallow-friends, who are gone when winter comes!

145:2 Those that make praise their constant work on earth shall have it their everlasting bliss in heaven.

145:3–5 We must declare, *Great is the Lord*, his presence infinite, his power irresistible, his brightness insupportable, his majesty awful, his dominion boundless, and his sovereignty incontestable; and therefore there is no dispute, but *great is the Lord*, and, if great, then *greatly to be praised*, with all that is within us, to the utmost of our power, and with all the circumstances of solemnity imaginable.

147:11 Our fear must save our hope from swelling into presumption, and our hope must save our fear from sinking into despair; thus must we take our work before us.

148:5 God created, and therefore may command; for he

commanded, and so created; his authority must always be acknowledged and acquiesced in, because he once spoke with such authority.

148:14 It is the greatest honour that can be put upon a man to be brought near to God, the nearer the better; and it will be best of all when nearest of all in the kingdom of glory.

150:2 Be not afraid of saying too much in the praises of God … all the danger is of saying too little.

150:6 The singing of birds is a sort of praising God. The brutes do in effect say to man, 'We would praise God if we could; do you do it for us.'

Proverbs

1:22 Sin is simplicity, and sinners are simple ones; they do foolishly, very foolishly; and the condition of those is very bad who love simplicity, are fond of their simple notions of good and evil, their simple prejudices against the ways of God, and are in their element when they are doing a simple thing, sporting themselves in their own deceivings and flattering themselves in their wickedness.

3:9–10 If we make our worldly estates serviceable to our religion we shall find our religion very serviceable to the prosperity of our worldly affairs.

3:24 The way to have a good night is to keep a good conscience; and the sleep, as of the labouring man, so of the wise and godly man, is sweet.

4:18 The saints will not be perfect till they come to heaven, but there they shall themselves *shine as the sun when he goes forth in his strength,* Matt. 13:43. Their graces and joys shall be all consummate. Therefore it is our wisdom to keep close to *the path of the just.*

5:8 Those that would be kept from harm must keep out of harm's way. Such tinder there is in the corrupt nature that it is madness, upon any pretence whatsoever, to come near the sparks.

6:29 *He that goes in to his neighbour's wife*, however he holds himself, God will not hold him guiltless. The fire of lust kindles the fire of hell.

8:34 While we have God's works before our eyes, and his word in our hand, we may be every day hearing Wisdom, and learning instruction from her.

9:17–18 Thus does Solomon show the hook; those that believe him will not meddle with the bait.

11:1 Nothing is more offensive to God than deceit in commerce. Nothing is more pleasing to God than fair and honest dealing.

11:30 Those that would win souls have need of wisdom to know how to deal with them; and those that do win souls show that they are wise.

12:3 Those that by faith are rooted in Christ are firmly fixed; in him their comfort and happiness are so rooted as never to be rooted up.

13:4 The slothful … desire the gains which the diligent get, but they hate the pains which the diligent take.

13:11 That which is won ill will never wear well, for a curse attends it which will waste it … That which is got by industry and honesty will grow more, instead of growing less; it will be a maintenance; it will be an inheritance; it will be an abundance.

14:12 Self-deceivers will prove in the end self-destroyers.

14:13 Spiritual joy is seated in the soul; the joy of the hypocrite is but from the teeth outward.

14:14 It is the evil heart of unbelief that departs from God; and of all sinners backsliders will have most terror when they reflect on *their own ways*, Luke 11:26. The happiness of the saints will be an eternal satisfaction in their graces, as tokens of and qualifications for God's peculiar favour. As sinners never think they have sin enough till it brings them to hell, so saints never think they have grace enough till it brings them to heaven.

14:29 A mild patient man is really to be accounted an intelligent man, one that learns of Christ, who is Wisdom itself.

14:33 Modesty is the badge of wisdom.

15:4 Hard words indeed break no bones, but many a heart has been broken by them.

15:13 Harmless mirth is recommended to us, as that which contributes to the health of the body, making men lively and fit for business, and to the acceptableness of the conversation, making the face to shine and rendering us pleasant one to another. A cheerful spirit, under the government of wisdom and grace, is a great ornament to religion, puts a further lustre upon the beauty of holiness, and makes men the more capable of doing good.

15:31 Those that learn well, and obey well, are likely in time to teach well and rule well.

15:32 The fundamental error of sinners is undervaluing their own souls; therefore they neglect to provide for them, abuse them, expose them, prefer the body before the soul, and wrong the soul to please the body.

16:7 The image of God appearing upon the righteous, and his particular lovingkindness to them, are enough to recommend them to the respect of all, even of those that have been most prejudiced against them.

16:16 Heavenly wisdom is better than worldly wealth, and to be preferred before it. Grace is more valuable than gold. Grace is the gift of God's peculiar favour; gold only of common providence. Grace is for ourselves; gold for others. Grace is for the soul and eternity; gold only for the body and time. Grace will stand us in stead in a dying hour, when gold will do us no good.

17:6 Those are unnatural children who reckon their aged parents a burden to them, and think they live too long; whereas, if the children be wise and good, it is as much their honour as can be that thereby they are comforts to their parents in the unpleasant days of their old age.

17:22 It is a great mercy that God gives us leave to be cheerful and cause to be cheerful, especially if by his grace he gives us hearts to be cheerful. But, if mirth be a medicine (understand it of diversion and recreation), it must be used sparingly, only when there is occasion, not turned into food, and it must be used medicinally, and by rule.

18:9 He that is trifling and careless in praying and hearing is brother to him that does not pray or hear at all; and omissions of duty and in duty are as fatal to the soul as commissions of sin.

18:17 We must ... remember that we have two ears, to hear both sides before we give judgment.

18:18 If the law be a lottery (as some have called it), it were as well that a lottery were the law.

18:24 Christ is a friend to all believers that *sticks closer than a brother*; to him therefore let them show themselves friendly.

19:13 That man has an uncomfortable life, and has need of a great deal of wisdom and grace to enable him to bear his afflictions and do his duty, who has a sot for his son and a scold for his wife.

20:1 *When the wine is in the wit is out*, and then the man, according as his natural temper is, either mocks like a fool or rages like a madman. Drunkenness, which pretends to be a sociable thing, renders men unfit for society, for it makes them abusive with their tongues and outrageous in their passions (Prov. 23:29).

20:16 Strange women have strange ways of impoverishing men to enrich themselves.

21:14 Covetousness is commonly a master-sin and has the command of other lusts.

21:17 Many a beau becomes a beggar.

22:15 There is a knot tied between the soul and sin, a true lover's knot; they two become one flesh.

23:5 The covetous man sits hatching upon his wealth, and brooding over it, till it is fledged, as the young ones under the hen, and then it is gone.

Snow will last awhile, and look pretty, if it be left to lie on the ground where it fell, but, if gathered up and laid in the bosom, it is dissolved and gone immediately.

23:9 If what a wise man says in his wisdom will not be heard, let him hold his peace, and try whether the wisdom of that will be regarded.

23:23 Riches should be employed for the getting of knowledge, rather than knowledge for the getting of riches.

26:20 Contention is as a fire; it heats the spirit, burns up all that is good, and puts families and societies into a flame.

27:7 Hunger is the best sauce. Coarse fare, with a good appetite to it, has a sensible pleasantness in it, which those are strangers to whose hearts are *overcharged with surfeiting*. ... The Virgin Mary seems to refer to this when she says (Luke 1:53), *The hungry*, who know how to value God's blessings, *are filled with good things*, but *the rich*, who despise them, are justly *sent empty away*.

27:15 The contentions of a neighbour may be like a sharp shower, troublesome for the time, yet, while it lasts, one may take shelter; but *the contentions of a wife* are like a constant soaking rain, for which there is no remedy but patience.

28:3 The hungry leech and the dry sponge suck most.

28:13 When we set sin before our face (as David, *My sin is ever before me*) God casts it behind his back.

29:6 Those that make God their chief joy have him for their exceeding joy, and it is their own fault if they do not *rejoice evermore*. If there be any true joy on this side heaven, doubtless those have it whose conversation is in heaven.

29:18 How bare does a place look without Bibles and ministers, and what an easy prey is it to the enemy of souls!

30:19 The kingdom of nature is full of wonders, marvellous things which the God of nature does, *past finding out*.

31:6–7 Wine is a cordial, and therefore to be used for want and not for wantonness, by those only that need cordials, as Timothy, who is advised to *drink a little wine*, only *for his stomach's sake and his often infirmities*, 1 Tim. 5:23.

31:9 Some observe that only wise men *open* their mouths, for fools have their mouths always open, are full of words.

31:10 A *virtuous woman* is a woman of spirit, who has the command of her own spirit and knows how to manage other people's, one that is pious and industrious, and a help meet for a man.

31:18 It is a mercy to have a candle-light to supply the want of day-light, and a duty, having that advantage, to improve it.

Ecclesiastes

1:4 We may give God the glory of that constant succession of generations, in which the world has hitherto had its existence, and will have to the end of time, admiring his patience in continuing that sinful species and his power in continuing that dying species.

1:14 He *saw all the works that were done under the sun*, works of nature in the upper and lower world, all within this vortex (to use the modern gibberish) which has the sun for its centre, works of art, the product of men's wit, in a personal or social capacity.

1:17 There is so much care in the contrivance of our worldly business, so much toil in the prosecution of it, and so much trouble in the disappointments we meet with in it, that we may well say, It is *vexation of spirit* to the wise observer of them.

1:17–18 The more we know, the more we see of our own ignorance.

2:1–2 Laughter and pleasure (says Sir William Temple) come from very different affections of the mind; for, as men have no disposition to laugh at things they are most pleased with, so they are very little pleased with many things they laugh at.

3:12 Every man's life is his opportunity of doing that which will make for him in eternity.

3:21 The soul of a beast is, at death, like a candle blown out—there is an end of it; whereas the soul of a man is then like a candle taken out of a dark lantern, which leaves the lantern useless indeed, but does itself shine brighter.

3:22 When we are gone it is likely we shall not see what is after us; there is no correspondence we know of between the other world and this, Job 14:21. Those in the other world will be wholly taken up with that world, so that they will not care for seeing what is done in this.

4:10 A monastic life then was surely never intended for a state of perfection, nor should those be reckoned the greatest lovers of God who cannot find in their hearts to love any one else.

4:12 Christ will by his Spirit come to them, and make the third, as he joined himself to the two disciples going to Emmaus, and then there is *a threefold cord* that can never be *broken. They that dwell in love, dwell in God, and God in them.*

5:2 It is not enough that what we say comes from the heart, but it must come from a composed heart, and not from a sudden heat or passion.

5:2–3 As confused dreams, frightful and perplexed, and such as disturb the sleep, are an evidence of a hurry of business which fills our head, so many words and hasty ones, used in prayer, are an evidence of folly reigning in the heart, ignorance of and unacquaintedness with both God and ourselves, low thoughts of God, and careless thoughts of our own souls.

5:10 Natural desires are at rest when that which is desired is obtained, but corrupt desires are insatiable. Nature is content with little, grace with less, but lust with nothing.

6:9 He is much happier that is always content, though he has ever so little, than he that is always coveting, though he has ever so much.

7:1 *A good name is* better *than* all *riches* (Prov. 22:1), that is, a name for wisdom and goodness with those that are wise and good—*the memory of the just*. Christ paid Mary for her ointment with a *good name*, a name in the gospels (Matt. 26:13), and we are sure he always pays with advantage.

7:10 We are not to think there is any universal decay in nature, or degeneracy in morals. God has been always good, and men always bad; and if, in some respects, the times are now worse than they have been, perhaps in other respects they are better.

9:7 Thy religious services, when performed with holy joy, are pleasing to God ... he loves to have his servants sing at their work, it proclaims him a good master.

9:9 Love thy wife; and *the wife whom thou lovest* thou wilt be likely to *live joyfully with*. Live with thy wife, and delight in her society. *Live joyfully with her*, and be most cheerful when thou art with her.

9:10 We must up and be doing now with all possible diligence, because our doing-time will be done shortly and we know not how soon. But this we know that, if the work of life be not done when our time is done, we are undone for ever.

11:4 Winds and clouds are in God's hands, are designed to try us, and our Christianity obliges us to endure hardness.

12:3 Moses was a rare instance of one who, when 120 years old, had good eye-sight, but ordinarily the sight decays in old people as soon as any thing, and it is a mercy to them that art helps nature with spectacles.

12:7 Man is a strange sort of creature, a ray of heaven united to a clod of earth; at death these are separated, and each goes to the place whence it came. Let us not therefore indulge the appetites of the body, nor pamper it (it will be worms' meat shortly), nor let *sin reign in our mortal bodies*, for they are mortal, Rom. 6:12. The soul does not die with the body. It goes *to God* as a Judge, to give account of itself, and to be lodged either with *the spirits in prison* (1 Peter 3:19) or with *the spirits in paradise* (Luke 23:43), according to what was done in the body.

12:13 The root of religion is fear of God reigning in the heart, and a reverence of his majesty, a deference to his authority, and a dread of his wrath.

Song of Solomon

Intro. As David's songs are many of them level to the capacity of the meanest, and there are shallows in them in which a lamb may wade, so this of Solomon's will exercise the capacities of the most learned, and there are depths in it in which an elephant may swim.

1:1 Solomon's songs were a thousand and five (1 Kings 4:32); those that were of other subjects are lost, but this of seraphic love remains, and will to the end of time.

1:4 See how the doctrine of special and effectual grace consists with our duty, and is a powerful engagement and encouragement to it, and yet reserves all the glory of all the good that is in us to God only.

2:3 Jesus is *gracious* (1 Peter 2:3); his *fruits* are all the precious privileges of the new covenant, purchased by his blood and communicated by his Spirit. Promises are sweet to a believer, yea, and precepts too. *I delight in the law of God after the inward man.* Pardons are sweet, and peace of conscience is sweet, assurances of God's love, joys of the Holy Ghost, the hopes of eternal life, and the present earnests and foretastes of it are sweet, all sweet to those that have their spiritual senses exercised.

2:16 It is the undoubted character of all true believers that they are Christ's, and then, and then only, he is theirs. They have given their own selves to him (2 Cor. 8:5); they receive his doctrine and obey his laws; they bear his image and espouse his interest; they belong to Christ. If we be his, his wholly, his only, his for ever, we may take the comfort of his being ours.

4:8–14 And so ought men to love their wives as Christ loves the church, and takes pleasure in it as if it were spotless and had no fault, when yet it is compassed with infirmity.

4:11 In the word of God there is sweet and wholesome nourishment, milk for babes, honey for those that are grown up. Christ is well-pleased with those that are full of his word.

4:16 We ought therefore to wait upon the Spirit of grace for his quickening influences, to pray for them, and to lay our souls under them. God has promised to give us his Spirit, but he will for this be enquired of.

5:2–3 He sues for entrance who may demand it; he knocks who could easily knock the door down. Those put a great contempt upon Christ that cannot find in their hearts to bear a cold blast for him, or get out of a warm bed.

5:6 Those that make Christ their beloved shall have him their friend; he has been, is, and will be, a special friend to all believers. '*This is my beloved and this is my friend* … others may do as they please, but this is my soul's choice, my soul's rest, my joy, my all; this is he whom I desire to live and die with.'

6:2–3 Drooping Christians would find benefit themselves by talking of Christ, as well as do good to others.

8:5 We must go up from the wilderness of this world having our conversation in heaven; and, at death, we must remove thither, *leaning* upon Christ, must live and die by faith in him. *To me to live is Christ*, and it is he that is gain in death.

Isaiah to Lamentations

Isaiah

4:3–4 All that are chosen to salvation are chosen to sanctification.

5:8 They would swell so big as to fill all space, and yet are still unsatisfied (Eccles. 5:10), as Alexander [the Great], who, when he fancied he had conquered the world, wept because he had not another world to conquer.

5:12 The use of music is lawful in itself; but when it is excessive, when we set our hearts upon it, misspend time in it, so that it crowds our spiritual and divine pleasures and draws away the heart from God, then it turns into sin to us.

5:15 It becomes those to look low that must shortly be laid low.

6:8 None are allowed to go for God but those who are sent by him.

7:9 The grace of faith is absolutely necessary to the quieting and composing of the mind in the midst of all the tosses of this present time (2 Chr. 20:20).

8:1 It is sometimes a good help to memory to put much matter in few words, which serve as handles by which we take hold of more.

8:16 As a testimony it directs our faith; as a law it directs our practice; and we ought both to subscribe to the truths of it and to submit to the precepts of it.

12:1 God sometimes brings his people into a wilderness that there he may *speak comfortably to them.*

14:23 When a people have nothing among them but dirt and filth, and will not be made clean with the besom of reformation, what can they expect but to be swept off the face of the earth with the besom of destruction?

16:11–12 Let us always rejoice with a holy trembling, rejoice as though we rejoiced not.

19:4 There is that in God which is a shelter and refreshment to his people in all weathers and arms them against the inconveniences of every change. Is the weather cool? There is that in his favour which will warm them. Is it hot? There is that in his favour which will cool them. Great men have their winter-house and their summer-house (Amos 3:15); but those that are at home with God have both in him.

19:15 The flourishing of a kingdom depends much upon the industry of the people; and *then* things are likely to do well when all hands are at work, when the head and top-branch do not disdain to labour, and the labour of the tail and rush is not disdained. But when the learned professions are unemployed, the principal merchants have no stocks, and the handicraft tradesmen have nothing to do, poverty comes upon a people *as one that travaileth* and *as an armed man*.

21:10 The corn of God's floor must expect to be threshed by afflictions and persecutions.

24:3 Sin has turned the earth *upside down*; the earth has become quite a different thing to man from what it was when God made it to be his habitation.

25:5 If the labourers in God's vineyard be at any time called to *bear the burden and the heat of the day*, he will find some way or other to refresh them, as with the shadow of a cloud, that they may not be pressed above measure.

26:2 Good principles fixed in the head will produce good resolutions in the heart and good practices in the life.

26:8 Even in the darkest night of affliction our desires must be towards God, as our sun and shield; for, however God is pleased to deal with us, we must never think the worse of him, nor cool in our love to him.

26:19 If we believe the resurrection of the dead, of our dead bodies at the last day, as Job did, and the prophet here, that will facilitate our belief of the promised restoration of the church's lustre and strength in this world.

28:1–8 It bodes ill to any people when so sottish a sin as drunkenness has become national.

28:9–10 Teachers should accommodate themselves to the capacity of the learners, give them what they most need and can best bear, and a little at a time (Deut. 6:6–7).

28:11 The apostle quotes it as a favour (1 Cor. 14:21), applying it to the gift of tongues, and complaining that yet for all this they would not hear.

28:11–12 Those that will not hear the comfortable voice of God's word shall be made to hear the dreadful voice of his rod.

28:23–29 The advancing of the art of husbandry is a common service to mankind more than the cultivating of most other arts. The skill of the husbandman is from God, as every good and perfect gift is. God's church is his husbandry (1 Cor. 3:9). Does not God by his ministers break up the fallow ground? Afflictions are God's threshing instruments, designed to loosen us from the world.

32:2 As the covert, and the hiding-place, and the rock, do themselves receive the battering of the wind and storm, to save those from it that take shelter in them, so Christ bore the storm himself to keep it off from us.

33:2 We must therefore every morning commit ourselves to him, and go forth in his strength to do the work of the day in its day.

35:8 Holiness is the rectitude of the human nature and will, in conformity to the divine nature and will. The way of holiness is that course of religious duties in which men ought to walk and press forward with an eye to the glory of God and their own felicity in the enjoyment of him. The *way of holiness* is the way of God's commandments; it is (as highways usually are) the *good old way* (Jer. 6:16).

38:1 Our being ready for death will make it come never the sooner, but much the easier: and those that are fit to die are most fit to live.

38:6 A good man cannot take much comfort in his own health and prosperity unless withal he see the welfare and prosperity of the church of God.

43:16 He that made dry land in the waters can produce waters in the driest land.

44:26 The exact fulfilling of the prophecies of scripture is a confirmation of the truth of the whole book and an incontestable evidence of its divine origin and authority.

46:6–7 How does the profuseness of idolaters shame the niggardliness of many who call themselves God's servants but are for a religion that will cost them nothing!

46:11 Though God has many things in his purposes which are not in his prophecies, he has nothing in his prophecies but what are in his purposes.

47:2 Let those that have power use it with temper and moderation, considering that the spoke which was uppermost will be under.

47:13 I confess I see not how the judicial astrology which some now pretend to, by the rules of which they undertake to prophesy concerning things to come, can be distinguished from that of the Chaldeans, nor therefore how it can escape the censure and contempt which this text lays under; yet I fear there are some who study their almanacs, and regard them and their prognostications, more than their Bibles and the prophecies there.

47:15 Happy are those who by faith and prayer deal with one that will be a *very present help in time of trouble*!

49:16 Some apply his engraving his church on the palms of his hands to the wounds in Christ's hands when he was crucified; he will look on the marks of them, and remember those for whom he suffered and died.

49:21–22 Let all that are concerned about young converts, and young beginners in religion, learn hence to deal very tenderly and carefully with them, as Christ does with the lambs which he *gathers with his arms and carries in his bosom*.

51:8 Clouds darken the sun, but give no obstruction to his progress.

53:10 While the world stands Christ will have a church in it, which he himself will be the life of.

54:15–17 We may with the greatest assurance depend upon God for the safety of his church.

55:7 Repentance, if it be true, strikes at the root, and washes the heart from wickedness.

57:1 Righteousness delivers from the sting of death, but not from the stroke of it. It is a sign that God intends war when he calls home his ambassadors.

57:2 Their souls then enter into peace, into the world of peace, where peace is in perfection and where there is no trouble. *Enter thou into the joy of thy Lord*.

Note, the grave is a bed of rest to all the Lord's people; there they rest from all their labours (Rev. 14:13). And the more weary they were the more welcome will be that rest to them (Job 3:17). It is a bed out of which they shall rise refreshed in the morning of the resurrection.

57:15 He that dwells in the highest heavens dwells in the lowest hearts and inhabits sincerity as surely as he inhabits eternity.

57:17 See also how insufficient afflictions of themselves are to reform men, unless God's grace work with them.

58:6 *Break every yoke*; not only let go those that are wrongfully kept under the yoke, but break the yoke of slavery itself, that it may not serve again another time nor any be made again to serve under it.

58:13 This law of the sabbath is still binding to us on our Lord's day.

59:4 *None calls for justice*, none complains of the violation of the sacred laws of justice, nor seeks to right those that suffer wrong or get the laws put in execution against vice and profaneness, and those lewd practices which are the shame, and threaten to be the bane, of the nation. Note, When justice is not done there is blame to be laid not only upon the magistrates that should administer justice, but upon the people that should call for it.

59:9–10 Those that love darkness rather than light shall have their doom accordingly.

59:21 Whatever is pretended to be a dictate of the Spirit must be tried by the scriptures. On these foundations the church is built, stands firmly, and shall stand for ever, Christ himself being the chief corner-stone.

61:3 *Beauty for ashes*. Here is an elegant *paronomasia* [play on words] in the original: He will give them *pheer—beauty*, for *epher—ashes*; he will turn their sorrow into joy as quickly and easily as you can transpose a letter; for he speaks, and it is done.

61:11 Though it may sometimes be winter with the church, when those blessings seem to wither and do not appear, yet the root of them is fixed, a spring-time will come, when through the reviving beams of the approaching Sun of righteousness they shall flourish again.

62:6 Ministers are watchmen on the church's walls, for it is a city besieged, whose concern it is to have sentinels on the walls, to take notice and give notice of the motions of the enemy. It is necessary that, as watchmen, they be wakeful, and faithful, and willing to endure hardness. They must never hold their peace; they must take all opportunities to give warning to sinners, in season, out of season, and must never betray the cause of Christ by a treacherous or cowardly silence. They must never hold their peace at the throne of grace; they must *pray and not faint*, as Moses lifted up his hands and kept them steady, till Israel had obtained the victory over Amalek (Exod. 17:10, 12).

62:11 Christ is not only the Saviour, but the salvation itself; for the happiness of believers is not only from him, but in him.

63:10 See the folly of sinners; they wilfully lose him for a friend who is the most desirable friend, and make him their enemy who is the most formidable enemy.

64:7 To pray is to *take hold of God*, by faith to take hold of the promises and declarations God has made of his good-will to us and plead them with him. Those that would take hold of God in prayer so as to prevail with him must stir up themselves to do it; all that is within us must be employed in the duty (and all little enough), our thoughts fixed and our affections flaming.

66:23 Christ is our temple, in whom by faith all believers meet.

Jeremiah

1:11–13 *What seest thou?* Prophets must have eyes in their heads as well as tongues, must be seers as well as speakers.

1:17 The fear of God is the best antidote against the fear of man.

2:26 *So are the house of Israel ashamed*, not with a penitent shame for the sin they had been guilty of, but with a penal shame for the disappointment they met with in that sin.

3:7 It is serious piety that God stands more upon than even his own rituals.

5:24 In harvest mercies therefore God is to be acknowledged, his power, and goodness, and faithfulness, for they all come from him. And it is a good reason why we should fear him, that we may keep ourselves in his love, because we have such a necessary dependence upon him. The fruitful seasons were witnesses for God, even to the heathen world, sufficient to leave them inexcusable in their contempt of him (Acts 14:17).

5:31 *What will you do in the end thereof?* Those that walk in bad ways would do well to consider the tendency of them both to greater sin and utter ruin. An end will come; the end of a wicked life will come, when it will be all called over again, and without doubt will be bitterness in the latter end.

6:16 Ask for the *old paths*, the paths prescribed by the law of God, the written word, that true standard of antiquity. Ask for the paths that the patriarchs travelled in before you, Abraham, and Isaac, and Jacob; and as you hope to inherit the promises made to them, tread in their steps. Note, The way of religion and godliness is a good old way, the way that all the saints in all ages have walked in. You will find that your walking in that way will be easy and pleasant; you will enjoy both your God and yourselves, and the way will lead you to true rest.

6:25 Let this remind us, when we travel the roads in safety and there is none to make us afraid, to bless God for our share in the public tranquillity.

8:22 If sinners die of their wounds, their blood is upon their own heads. The blood of Christ is balm in Gilead, his Spirit is the physician there, both sufficient, all sufficient, so that they might have been healed, but would not.

9:24 We may *glory in this*, that, wherever we are, we have an acquaintance with and an interest in a God that *exercises lovingkindness, and judgment, and righteousness in the earth*, that is not only just to all his creatures and will do no wrong to any of them, but kind to all his children and will protect them and provide for them.

10:2 God would not have his people to be *dismayed at the signs of heaven*, to reverence the stars as deities, nor to frighten themselves with any prognostications grounded upon them. Let them fear the God of heaven, and keep up a reverence of his providence, and then they need not be *dismayed at the signs of heaven*, for the *stars in their courses* fight not against any that are at peace with God.

10:14 *Every founder* is himself *confounded by the graven image*; when he has made it by a mistake, he is more and more confirmed in his mistake by it; he is bewildered, bewitched, and cannot disentangle himself from the snare.

10:19 When I am in affliction I should say, 'This is an evil, and I will bear it, because it is the will of God that I should, because his wisdom has appointed this for me and his grace will make it work for good to me.'

10:23 It is some comfort to poor ministers that, if men will not hear them, God will; and to him they have liberty of access at all times. Let them close their preaching with prayer, as the prophet, and then they shall have no reason to say that they have laboured in vain.

12:2 He spoke by the Spirit of prophecy, without which it is not safe to charge men with hypocrisy whose appearances are plausible.

14:22 The sovereignty of God should engage, and his all-sufficiency encourage, our attendance on him and our expectations from him at all times.

17:5–6 Cleaving to the cistern is leaving the fountain, and is resented accordingly.

17:7–8 Observe the duty required of us to *trust in the Lord*, to do our duty to him and then depend upon him to bear us out in doing it. It is to *make the Lord our hope*, his favour the good we hope for and his power the strength we hope in. He that does so shall be *as a tree planted by the waters* ... which denotes both the establishment and the comfort which those have who make God their hope; they are easy, they are pleasant, and enjoy a continual security and serenity of mind.

17:14 Those that come to God to be healed ought to be abundantly satisfied in the all-sufficiency of their physician. *Save me*, and *then I shall* certainly *be saved*, be my dangers and enemies ever so threatening. If God holds us up, we shall live; if he protects us, we shall be safe.

20:9, 13 It was the lively exercise of faith that turned his sighs into songs and his tremblings into triumphs. It is proper to express our hope in God by our praising him, and our praising God by our singing to him.

22:10 Dying saints may be justly envied, while living sinners are justly pitied.

22:14 Those therefore that are enlarging their houses, and making them more sumptuous, have need to look well to the frame of their own spirits in the doing of it, and carefully to watch against the workings of vain-glory.

22:15 Those children that despise their parents' old fashions commonly come short of their real excellences.

22:16 The right knowledge of God consists in doing our duty, particularly that which is the duty of our place and station in the world.

22:18–19 It was Jehoiakim's pride that he had built a fine house, but Josiah's true praise that he kept a good house.

23:1–2 Here is a word of terror to the negligent shepherds. In not visiting them, and doing their duty to them, they did in effect scatter them and drive them away.

23:6 As Mediator, he is *our righteousness*. By making satisfaction to the justice of God for the sin of man, he has brought in an everlasting righteousness, and so made it over to us in the covenant of grace that, upon our believing consent to that covenant, it becomes ours.

23:26 Pretences to new revelation may prove as dangerous to religion as the denying of all revelation.

27:16, 22 We are apt to set our clock before God's dial, and then to quarrel because they do not agree; but the Lord is a God of judgment, and it is fit that we should wait for him.

29:12–14 When God is about to give his people the expected good he pours out a spirit of prayer, and it is a good sign that he is coming towards them in mercy. Then when you see the *expected end* approaching, *then you shall call upon me*. Note, Promises are given, not to supersede, but to quicken and encourage prayer: and when deliverance is coming we must by prayer go forth to meet it.

30:14–15 Instead of repining, thou shouldst be repenting. The issue will be good at last, and therefore *rejoice in hope*.

31:9 Weeping and praying do well together; tears put life into prayers ... and prayers help to wipe away tears.

31:15–16 Though we mourn, we must not murmur, nor must we resolve, as Jacob did, to go to the grave mourning.

32:39–40 As it is God's prerogative to fashion men's hearts, so it is his promise to his people to fashion theirs aright; and a heart to fear God is indeed a good heart, and well fashioned. Teachers may put good things into our heads, but it is God only that can put them into our hearts.

We cannot better consult the good of posterity than by setting up, and keeping up, the fear and worship of God in our families.

36:3 The conversion of sinners from their evil courses is that which ministers should aim at in preaching; and people hear the word in vain if that point be not gained with them.

37:20 A lion in God's cause must be a lamb in his own.

39:14 God's people and ministers have often found fairer and kinder usage among strangers and infidels than among those that call themselves of the holy city.

42:3 In every difficult doubtful case our eye must be up to God for direction. They then might expect to be directed by a *spirit of prophecy*, which has now ceased; but we may still in faith pray to be guided by a *spirit of wisdom* in our hearts and the hints of Providence.

44:27 To those whom God finds impenitent sinners he will be found an implacable Judge.

48:36 Riches are shedding things, and, like dust as they are, slip through our fingers even when we are in most care to hold them fast and grip them hard.

49:11 It is an unspeakable comfort to the people of God, when they are dying, that they may leave their surviving relations with

God, may, in faith, commit them to him; and though they cannot promise themselves great things in the world for them, yet they may hope that he will preserve them alive, always, provided that they trust in him.

Lamentations

3:22 When our comforts fail, yet God's compassions do not. Whatever hard things we suffer, we must never entertain any hard thoughts of God, but must still be ready to own that he is both kind and faithful.

3:31–32 When we are cast down, yet we are not cast off.

3:33 He never afflicts us but when we give him cause to do it. He does not dispense his frowns as he does his favours, *ex mero motu—from his mere good pleasure*.

He delights not in the death of sinners, or the disquiet of saints, but punishes with a kind of reluctance.

He comes out of his place to punish, for his place is the mercy-seat.

He retains his kindness for his people even when he afflicts them.

3:37 Men are but tools which the great God makes use of, and manages as he pleases, in the government of this lower world; and they cannot accomplish any of their designs without him.

3:39 While there is life there is hope, and therefore, instead of complaining that things are bad, we should encourage ourselves with the hope that they will be better.

3:56 Prayer is the breath of the new man, sucking in the air of mercy in petitions and returning it in praises; it is both the evidence and the maintenance of the spiritual life.

Ezekiel to Malachi

Ezekiel

1:4 Nothing is more easy than to determine that God is, nothing more difficult than to describe what he is.

2:6 No providences will of themselves humble and reform men, unless the grace of God work with them.

3:5–6 The apostles indeed were sent to *many people of a strange speech*, but they could not have done any good among them if they had not had *the gift of tongues*.

3:10–14 Those whom God calls to the ministry, as he furnishes their heads for it, so he bows their hearts to it.

3:23 We are not now to expect such visions.

3:24 Those that are called to preach must find time to study, and a great deal of time too, must often shut themselves up in their houses, that they may give attendance to reading and meditation, and so their profiting may appear to all.

4:7 We make use only of such signs as God himself has expressly appointed.

4:11 Nature is content with a little, grace with less, but lust with nothing.

6:9 Where God designs grace to repent he allows space to repent; yet many who have the space want the grace.

7:19 Money is no defence against the arrests of death, nor any alleviation to the miseries of the damned.

9:2 That way that sin lies, judgments may be expected to come.

9:4 It is not enough that we do not delight in the sins of others, and that we have not fellowship with them, but we must mourn for them, and lay them to heart; we must grieve for that which we cannot help, as those that hate sin for its own sake, and have a tender concern for the souls of others.

10:12 Events are not determined by the wheel of fortune, which is blind, but by the wheels of Providence, which are full of eyes.

11:16 '... yet will I be to them as a little sanctuary in the countries where they shall come.' Those at Jerusalem have the temple, but without God; those in Babylon have God, though without the temple.

14:9 We are sure that God is not the author of sin, but we are sure that he is the Lord of all and the judge of sinners, and that he often makes use of one wicked man to destroy another, and so of one wicked man to deceive another. Both are sins in him who does them, and so they are *not* from God; both are punishments to him to whom they are done, and so they *are* from God.

15:4 To burn anything for fuel which is good for other work is bad husbandry.

16:2–3 Ministers have need of one another's help both by preaching and writing.

16:17 It is God that gives us our gold and silver; the products of trade, of art and industry, are the gifts of God's providence to us, as well as the fruits of the earth. Every penny has God's image upon it as well as Caesar's.

17:2 God often used similitudes by his servants the prophets, and Christ himself *opened his mouth in parables* ... Note, Ministers should study to find out acceptable words, and try various methods to do good; and, as far as they have reason to think will be for edification, should both bring that which is familiar into their preaching and their preaching too into their familiar discourse, that there may be not so vast a dissimilitude as with some there is between what they say in the pulpit and what they say out.

17:7 See the folly of fretful discontented spirits, that ruin themselves by striving to better themselves, whereas they might be easy and happy enough if they would but *make the best of that which is*.

18:4 'All souls are mine'—God here claims a property in all the souls of the children of men, one as well as another. He that is the Maker of *all things* is in a particular manner the *Father of spirits*, for his image is stamped on the souls of men; it was so in their creation; it is so in their renovation.

18:10 As it was in the royal line of the kings of Judah, so it often happens in private families, that godly parents have wicked children and wicked parents have godly children.

21:21 In cases proper for an appeal to Providence it is sufficient that *the lot be cast into the lap*, with that prayer, *Give a perfect lot*, and a firm belief that the *disposal thereof* is not fortuitous, but *of the Lord*, Prov. 16:33.

22:12 For neighbours to gain by one another in a way of fair trading is well, but those who are *greedy of gain*, will not be held within the rules of equity.

24:1–2 It is good to keep an exact account of the date of remarkable occurrences, which may sometimes contribute to the manifesting of God's glory so much the more in them, and the explaining and confirming of scripture prophecies. *Known unto God are all his works.*

26:17 Those who have the world in their hearts lament the loss of great men more than the loss of good men.

27:3 It is a great convenience, upon many accounts, to live in an island; seas are the most *ancient landmark*, not *which our fathers have set*, but the God of our fathers, and which cannot be removed as other landmarks may, nor so easily got over.

27:12–25 It is the wisdom of a nation to encourage art and industry, and not to bear hard upon the handicraft-tradesmen; for it contributes much to the wealth and honour of a nation to send abroad *wares of their own making*, which may bring them in the *multitude of all riches*.

31:9 It is the unhappiness of those who in any thing excel others that thereby they make themselves the objects of envy; and *who can stand before envy*?

32:12 It is therefore our wisdom to be full of treasures in heaven.

32:16 By enlarging the matters of our joy we increase the occasions of our sorrow.

33:9 It is a comfort to ministers that they may through grace save themselves, though they cannot be instrumental to save so many as they wish of those that hear them.

33:31 Covetousness is the ruining sin of multitudes that make a great profession of religion; it is the love of the world that secretly eats the love of God out of their hearts.

36:23 Nor does any thing make a man truly great but being truly good, and partaking of God's holiness.

36:26–27 A promise of the Spirit, and his gracious influences and operations, which we have as much need of for our sanctification as we have of Christ's merit for our justification.

36:27 God does not force men to walk in his statutes by external violence, but causes them to walk in his statutes by an internal principle.

36:29, 34 God will *call for the corn* and yet they must *till the ground* for it. Note, Even promised mercies must be laboured for.

36:37 What is the matter of God's promises must be the matter of our prayers. Our communion with God must be kept up by the word and prayer in all the operations of his providence concerning us and in both he must be enquired of.

37:7, 10 God's grace can save souls without our preaching, but our preaching cannot save them without God's grace, and that grace must be sought by prayer.

40:3 The temple of God is built by line and rule ... the church is formed according to the scripture, *the pattern in the mount*. That is the line and measuring reed that is in the hand of Christ.

42:4 Man is made for society, and Christians for the communion of saints; and the duties of that communion we must make conscience of, and the privileges and pleasures of that communion we must take the comfort of.

44:24 Ministers must decide controversies according to the word of God, *to the law and to the testimony*.

45:25 See the necessity of our frequently repeating the same religious exercises. Though the sacrifice of atonement is offered *once for all*, yet the sacrifices of acknowledgment, that of a broken heart, that of a thankful heart, those spiritual sacrifices which are acceptable to God through Christ Jesus, must be every day offered. We should, as here, fall into a method of holy duties, and keep to it.

46:5, 7, 11 In works of piety God expects and requires but that we should do according to our ability, every man *as God has prepared him* (1 Cor. 16:2).

47:9 The grace of God makes dead sinners alive and living saints lively.

48:1–30 God, in the dispensation of his grace, does not follow the same method that he does in the disposals of his providence.

It was never the intention of the gospel to pluck up the hedge of property and lay all in common; it was in a way of charity, not of legal right, that the first Christians had all things in common (Acts 2:44), and many precepts of the gospel suppose that every man should know his own.

Daniel

1:8 How much better is it with those that retain their integrity in the depths of affliction than with those that retain their iniquity in the heights of prosperity!

1:13 People will not believe the benefit of abstemiousness and a spare diet, nor how much it contributes to the health of the body, unless they try it.

2:18 Though we cannot in faith pray for miracles, yet we may pray in faith to him who has all hearts in his hand, and who in his providence does wonders without miracles.

2:24 Since God shows common kindness to the evil and good, we should do so too, and be ready to save the lives even of bad men (Matt. 5:45).

3:1 Strong convictions often come short of a sound conversion.

3:5 This mirth and gaiety in the worship would be very agreeable to carnal sensual minds, that are strangers to that spiritual worship which is due to God who is a spirit.

3:7 That way that sense directs the most will go; there is nothing so bad which the careless world will not be drawn to by a concert of music, or driven to by a fiery furnace. And by such methods as these false worship has been set up and maintained.

3:15 Thus does the matter lie in a little compass—*Turn, or burn.* None of these things move them [Shadrach, Meshach and Abednego]; they are resolved rather to die in their integrity than live in their iniquity.

3:16 Those that would avoid sin must not parley with temptation.

4:12 The kings of the earth are to their subjects but as the shadow of a great tree; but Christ is to his subjects as the *shadow of a great rock* (Isa. 32:2). Nay, because that, though strong, may be cold, they are said to be hidden under the *shadow of his wings* (Ps. 17:8), where they are not only safe, but warm.

4:33 Let us learn how to value our own reason, and to pity the case of those that are under the prevailing power of melancholy or distraction, or are delirious, and to be very tender in our censures of them and conduct towards them, for it is a trial common to men, and a case which, some time or other, may be our own.

5:17 But let us do our duty in the world, do it all the real service we can, read God's writing to it in a profession of religion, and by an agreeable conversation make known the interpretation of it, and then trust God for his gifts, his rewards, in comparison with which all the world can give is mere trash and trifles.

6:18 The best way to have a good night is to keep a good conscience, then we may lie down in peace.

7:1 Ministers in their preaching are to *tell the sum of the matters* that are written.

7:28 If we would have God's word ready in our mouths when we have occasion for it, we must keep it in our hearts at all times.

9:3 God's promises are intended, not to supersede, but to excite and encourage, our prayers.

10:10, 16, 18 The hand of God's power going along with the word of his grace is alone effectual to redress all our grievances, and to rectify whatever is amiss in us.

10:17 Whenever we enter into communion with God it becomes us to have a due sense of the vast distance and disproportion that here are between us and the holy angels, and of the infinite distance, and no proportion at all, between us and the holy God.

11:20 Some have called great men the *foot-balls of fortune*; or, rather, they are the *tools of Providence*.

For the right understanding of some parts of scripture, it is necessary that heathen authors be consulted, which give light to the scripture, and show the accomplishment of what is there foretold; we have therefore reason to bless God for the human learning with which many have done great service to divine truths.

11:36 And here some think begins a prophecy of the antichrist, the papal kingdom.

12:5 The further we look into the things of God, and the more we converse with them, the more we shall see of those things, and still new discoveries will be made to us; those that know much, if they improve it, shall know more.

12:13 It is good for us all to think much of going away from this world ... We shall not go till God calls for us to another world, and till he has done with us in this world, till he says, '*Go thou thy way*' ... and leave it to others to take thy room.'

It is a comfort to all the saints, that whatever their lot is in the days of time, they shall have a happy lot in *the end of the days*, shall have their *lot among the chosen*.

A believing hope and prospect of a blessed lot in the heavenly Canaan at the end of the days, will be an effectual support to us when we are going our way out of this world, and will furnish us with living comforts in dying moments.

Hosea

1:7 The less there is of man in any salvation, and the more of God, the brighter it shines and the sweeter it tastes.

2:7 Whoever have exchanged the service of God for the service of the world and the flesh have, sooner or later, been made to own that they *changed for the worse*, and that while they continued in good company, and went on in the way of good duties, and made conscience how they spent their time and what they said or did, it was better with them; they had more true comfort and enjoyment of themselves than ever they had since they went astray.

2:10 Those who will not deliver themselves into the hand of God's mercy cannot be delivered out of the hand of his justice.

2:18 If the inferior creatures are thus laid under an engagement to serve us, it is our part of the covenant not to abuse them, but to serve God with them.

4:15 *The Lord liveth* ... Those that would be steady in their adherence to God must possess themselves with an awe and reverence of God, and always speak of him with solemnity and seriousness; for those that can make a jest of the true God will make a god of any thing.

4:17 Those that are not disturbed in their sin will be destroyed for their sin.

5:14 None can be delivered out of the hand of God's justice but those that are delivered into the hands of his grace. It is in vain for a man to strive with his Maker.

5:15 When men begin to complain more of their sins than of their afflictions then there begins to be some hope of them.

6:1 He that has torn will *heal us*, he that has smitten will *bind us up*, as the skilful surgeon with a tender hand binds up the broken bone or bleeding wound. Note, The same providence of God that afflicts his people relieves them, and the same Spirit of God that convinces the saints comforts them.

7:7 Those are not only heated with sin, but hardened in sin, that continue to live without prayer even when they are in trouble and distress.

7:14 Carnal hearts, in their prayers to God, covet temporal mercies only, and dread and deprecate no other but temporal judgments, for they have no sense of any other.

8:12 If those were happy who had the *great things of God's law* written to them, how much happier are we who have the much greater things of his gospel written to us!

9:15 Golgotha in Syriac is the same with Gilgal in Hebrew.

10:12 Seeking the Lord is to be every day's work, but there are some special occasions given by the providence and grace of God when it is, in a particular manner, time to seek him.

12:10 God keeps an account whether we do or no, of the sermons we hear; and those that have long enjoyed the means of grace in purity, plenty and power, that have been frequently, faithfully, and familiarly, told the mind of God, will have a great deal to answer for another day if they persist in a course of iniquity.

13:6 We ought to know that we live upon God when we live upon common providence, though we do not, as Israel in the wilderness, live upon miracles.

13:9 Those may justly be reckoned their own destroyers who defer and put off their own repentance, by which alone they might help themselves. Those are in danger of miscarrying in conversion who delay it, and will not put forth themselves to speed the work and bring it to an issue.

13:14 Those who, upon their repenting and believing, are, for the sake of Christ's righteousness, acquitted from the guilt of sin and saved from death and hell, which are the *wages of sin*, are those *ransomed of the Lord* that shall, in the great day, be brought out of the grave in triumph, and it shall be as impossible for the bands of death to hold them as it was to hold their Master.

14:1 Sin is a fall; and it concerns those that have fallen by sin to get up again by repentance.

14:5 Pardoning mercy is always accompanied with renewing grace.

Spiritual growth consists most in the growth of the root, which is out of sight.

14:9 The same sun softens wax and hardens clay.

Joel

1:5 The more delights we make necessary to our satisfaction the more we expose ourselves to trouble and disappointment.

2:22 The *creature*, that is now *made subject to vanity* and *groans* under it, *shall be brought*, though not into the glorious joy, yet *into the glorious liberty, of the children of God*, Rom. 8:21.

3:15 The damned sinners in hell shall not be allowed their light, for God himself will be *their everlasting light*, Isa. 60:19.

Amos

3:6 *Shall there be evil in a city*, in a family, in a nation, *and the Lord has not done it*, appointed it, and performed what he appointed? The evil of sin is from ourselves; it is our own doing. But the evil of trouble, personal or public, is from God, and is his doing; whoever are the instruments, God is the principal agent. *Out of his mouth both evil and good proceed.* This consideration, that, whatever evil is in the city, the Lord has done it, should engage us patiently to bear our share in public calamities and to study to answer God's intention in them.

God warns before he wounds.

3:15 The pomp or pleasantness of men's houses will be so far from fortifying them against God's judgments that it will make them the more grievous and vexatious, as their extravagance about them will be put to the score of their sins and follies.

4:3 Those who will not be kept within the hedge of God's precept forfeit the benefit of the hedge of God's protection.

8:2 The word that signifies *the end* is *ketz*, which is of near affinity with *kitz*, the word used for *summer-fruit*.

9:2 Hell itself, though it has its name in English from its being *hilled*, or *covered over*, or *hidden*, cannot hide them. Heaven, though it has its name from being *heaved*, or lifted up, shall not put them out of the reach of God's judgments; as hell cannot hide them, so heaven will not.

Obadiah

1:3 Sinners will certainly be made ashamed of their pride and security, of their pride when it has a fall and of their security when their confidences fail their expectation.

1:5 Treasures on earth, though ever so fast locked up and ever so artfully hidden, cannot be so safely laid up but that thieves may break through and steal; it is therefore our wisdom to *lay up for ourselves treasures in heaven.*

Jonah

3:4 We should be alarmed if we were sure not to live a month, and yet we are careless, though we are not sure to live a day.

4:9 Inordinate affection lays a foundation of inordinate affliction; what we are over-fond of when we have it we are apt to over-grieve for when we lose it, and we may see our folly in both.

Micah

1:1 What is written in the Bible, and what is preached by the ministers of Christ according to what is written there, must be heard and received, not as the word of dying men, which we may be judges of, but as the word of the living God, which we must be judged by, for so it is.

2:10 The world ... was designed for our passage, but not for our portion—our inn, but not our home.

2:12 Christ is the church's King; he is Jehovah.

3:11 It is very absurd for sinners to think that their impudence will be their impunity.

4:13 All we have must have *holiness to the Lord* written upon it, all our gain and substance must be *consecrated to the Lord of the whole earth*, Isa. 23:18.

5:2 Was not he *ruler in Israel* whom winds and seas obeyed, to whom legions of devils were forced to submit, and who commanded away diseases from the sick and called the dead out of their graves?

5:5 Christ is our peace as a priest, making atonement for sin, and reconciling us to God; and he is our peace as a king, conquering our enemies and commanding down disquieting fears and passions.

6:8 There is an innate goodness in moral duties ... they are not, as ceremonial observances, good because they are commanded, but commanded because they are good. Our conformity is not only the condition of our future happiness, but is a great expedient of our present happiness.

7:18 The pardon of sin is the foundation of all other covenant-mercies.

7:19 If God forgave the sin that has been committed by us, he will subdue the sin that dwells in us.

Nahum

2:6 The same word signifies both a palace and a temple. When the God of heaven goes forth to contend with a people, neither the palaces nor their kings, neither the temples nor their gods, can protect and shelter them, but must all inevitably fall with them.

3:16–17 It is rare to find even those that have shared with us in our joys willing to share with us in our griefs too.

Habakkuk

2:4 Those that are made *just by faith shall live*, shall be happy here and for ever; while they are here, they live by it; when they come to heaven faith shall be swallowed up in vision.

2:5 Those that will not be content with their allotments shall not have the comfort of their achievements.

Zephaniah

3:9 Converting grace refines the language, not by making the phrases witty, but the substance wise.

Haggai

1:2 Many a good work is put by by being put off, as Felix put off the prosecution of his convictions to a more convenient season. There is an aptness in us to misinterpret providential discouragements in our duty, as if they amounted to a discharge from our duty, when they are only intended for the trial and exercise of our courage and faith.

2:9 The purity of the church, and the strict adherence to divine institutions, are much more its glory than external pomp and splendour.

Zechariah

2:4 The city shall be in a manner lost in the suburbs, as London is, where the out-parishes are more populous than those within the walls.

3:1 When we stand before God to minister to him, or stand up for God to serve his interests, we must expect to meet with all the resistance that Satan's subtlety and malice can give us. Let us then resist him that resists us and he shall flee from us.

3:2 It is the happiness of the saints that the Judge is their friend; the same that they are accused to is their patron and protector, and an advocate for them, and he will be sure to bring them off. Satan is here checked by one that has authority, and that has conquered him, and many a time silenced him.

Note, Those that belong to Christ have him ready to appear vigorously for them when Satan appears most vehement against them. He does not parley with him, but stops his mouth immediately with this sharp reprimand: *The Lord rebuke thee, O Satan!* This is the best way of dealing with that furious enemy. *Get thee behind me, Satan.*

Narrow escapes from imminent danger are happy presages and powerful pleas for more eminent favours. A converted soul is a *brand plucked out of the fire* by a miracle of free grace, and therefore shall not be left to be a prey to Satan.

4:2 This candlestick had one *bowl*, or common receiver, on the top, into which oil was continually dropping, and from it, by seven secret pipes, or passages, it was diffused to the seven lamps, so that, without any further care, they received oil as fast as they wasted it (as in those which we call *fountain-ink-*

horns, or *fountain-pens*); they never wanted, nor were ever glutted, and so kept always burning clear.

8:4 Old age needs a support, and should not be ashamed to use it, but should furnish itself with divine graces, which will be the strength of the heart and a better support than a staff in the hand. It is a graceful thing to a city to see abundance of old people in it; it is a sign, not only of the healthfulness of the air, but of the prevalence of virtue and the suppression and banishment of those many vices which cut off the number of men's months in the midst; it is a sign not only that the climate is temperate, but that the people are so.

8:5 Their children shall be hearty and cheerful … It is their pleasant playing age; let us not grudge it to them; much good may it do them and no harm.

8:9 Those who lay their hands to the plough of duty shall have them strengthened with the promises of mercy.

10:1 We must ask for mercies in their proper time, and not expect that God should go out of his usual way and method for us.

12:3 Those that make a jest of religion, and banter sacred things, will find them a burdensome stone, that it is ill-jesting with edged-tools, and though they make light of it (saying, *Am I not in sport?*) they bring upon themselves an insupportable sinking load of guilt.

12:10 When God intends great mercy for his people the first thing he does is to set them a-praying.

13:7 Observe how he calls him, 'As God, he is *my fellow*'; for he thought it *no robbery to be equal with God*. He and *the Father* are *one*.

Malachi

1:10 In order to our acceptance with God it is not enough to do that which, for the matter of it, is good, but we must do it from a right principle, in a right manner, and for a right end.

2:7 It is an honour to God's servants to be employed as his messengers and to be sent on his errands. Angels have their names hence. Haggai was called *the Lord's messenger*.

People should not only seek comfort at the mouth of their ministers, but should seek the law there; for, if we be found in the way of duty, we shall find it the way of comfort.

2:9 As sin is a reproach to any people, so especially to priests; there is not a more despicable animal upon the face of the earth than a profane, wicked, scandalous minister.

2:10 Corrupt practices are the genuine fruit and product of corrupt principles.

3:1 By this it appears that the Messiah was to come while *that temple* was standing; that, therefore, being long since destroyed, we must conclude that he has come, and we are to look for no other.

3:8 God must be served in the first place, and our quota must be contributed for the support of religion in the place where we live, that God's name may be sanctified, and his kingdom may come, and his will be done, even before we provide our daily bread; for the interests of our souls ought to be preferred before those of our bodies.

3:17 The saints are God's jewels; they are highly esteemed by him and are dear to him; they are comely with the comeliness that he puts upon them, and he is pleased to glory in them; they are a *royal diadem* in his hand.

4:4–5 This is doubtless intended for a solemn conclusion, not only of this prophecy, but of the canon of the Old Testament, and is a plain information that they were not to expect any more sayings nor writings by divine inspiration, any more of the dictates of the Spirit of prophecy, till the beginning of the gospel of the Messiah, which sets aside the Apocrypha as no part of holy writ, and which therefore the Jews never received.

Matthew to Luke

Matthew

Preface What therefore I have endeavoured here has been with this view, to make these writings serviceable to the faith, holiness and comfort of good Christians.

1:1 Delays of promised mercies, though they exercise our patience, do not weaken God's promise.

1:3, 5–6 We ought not to upbraid people with the scandals of their ancestors; it is what they cannot help, and has been the lot of the best, even of our Master himself.

1:18 We may also learn, from this example, that it is good to enter into the married state with deliberation, and not hastily—to preface the nuptials with a contract. It is better to *take* time to consider before than to *find* time to repent after.

1:21 Those whom Christ saves he saves *from their sins*; from the guilt of sin by the *merit of his death*, from the dominion of sin by the *Spirit of his grace*.

1:23 By the light of *nature,* we see God as a God *above us*; by the light of the *law*, we see him as a God *against us*; but by the light of the gospel, we see him as *Immanuel*, God *with us*, in our own nature, and (which is more) in our nature. Herein the Redeemer *commended his love*.

2:2 Those in whose hearts the day-star is risen, to give them anything of the knowledge of Christ, must make it their business to worship him. Have we seen Christ's star? Let us study to give him honour.

2:9–10 If we go on as far as we can in the way of our duty, God will direct and enable us to do that which of ourselves we cannot do; *Up, and be doing, and the Lord will be with thee.*

2:13 Those that are spiritually related to Christ by faith have that communion and correspondence with Heaven which before they were strangers to.

2:16 By all the prophecies of the Old Testament it appears that Bethlehem was the place, and this the time, of Messiah's nativity; now all the children of Bethlehem, born at this time, being murdered, and Jesus only escaping, none but Jesus could pretend to be the Messiah.

3:1 John Baptist was a priest of the order of Aaron, yet we find him preaching in a *wilderness*, and never officiating in the *temple*; but Christ, who was not a son of Aaron is yet often found in the temple, and sitting there as one having authority; so it was foretold, Mal. 3:1. *The Lord whom ye seek shall suddenly come to his temple;* not the *messenger* that was to prepare his way. This intimated that the priesthood of Christ was to thrust out that of Aaron, and drive it into a wilderness.

3:3 John is called the *voice*, which is startling and awakening. Christ is called the *Word*, which, being distinct and articulate, is more instructive. John, as the *voice*, roused men, and then Christ, as the *Word*, taught them; as we find, Rev. 14:2.

3:4 A conviction of the vanity of the world, and everything in it, is the best preparative for the entertainment of the kingdom of heaven in the heart. *Blessed are the poor in spirit.*

3:14 Ministers, who preach to others, and baptize others, are concerned to look to it that they preach to themselves, and be themselves baptized with the Holy Ghost. Take heed to thyself first; *save thyself*, 1 Tim. 4:16.

3:15 No pretence of humility must make us decline our duty.

4:1 The Devil has a particular spite at useful persons, who are not only good, but given to do good, especially at their first setting out. Let young ministers know what to expect, and arm accordingly.

Temptations, if not yielded to, are not sins, they are afflictions only, and such as may be the lot of those with whom God is well-pleased.

4:4 This is observable, that Christ answered and baffled all the temptations of Satan with, *It is written.* He is himself the eternal Word, and could have produced the mind of God without having recourse to the writings of Moses; but he put honour upon the scripture, and, to set us an example, he appealed to what was written in the law. This method we must take when at any time we are tempted to sin; resist and repel the temptation with, *It is written.* The word of God is *the sword of the Spirit.* The only offensive weapon in all the Christian armoury (Eph. 6:17); and we may say of it as David of Goliath's sword, *None is like that* in our spiritual conflicts.

4:5 God casts down, that he may raise up; the Devil raises up, that he may cast down: therefore they who would take heed of *falling* must take heed of *climbing*. High places *in the church* are, in a special manner, dangerous. They who excel in gifts, who are in eminent stations, and have gained great reputation, have need to keep humble; for Satan will be sure to aim at them, to puff them up with pride, that they may *fall into the condemnation of the Devil.* Those that *stand high* are concerned to *stand fast.*

4:6 The Devil said, *Cast thyself down.* The Devil could not cast him down, though a little thing would have done it, from the top of a spire.

We must never promise ourselves any more than God has promised us.

4:9 The best of saints may be tempted to the worst of sins,

especially when they are under the power of melancholy; as, for instance, to atheism, blasphemy, murder, self-murder, and what not. This is their affliction, but while there is no consent to it, nor approbation of it, it is not their sin; Christ was tempted to worship Satan.

4:16 When the gospel comes, light comes; when it comes to any place, when it comes to any soul, it makes day there, John 3:19; Luke 1:78–79. Light is discovering, it is directing; so is the gospel.

4:18 It is the honour and comfort of a house, when those that are of the *same* family, are of *God's* family.

4:19–20 In all his preaching he gave a common call to all the country, but in this he gave a special and particular call to those that were given him by the Father. Let us see and admire the power of Christ's grace, own his word to be the rod of his strength, and wait upon him for those powerful influences which are necessary to the efficacy of the gospel call—those distinguishing influences.

4:21 Ministers should be always employed, either in teaching or studying; they may always find themselves something to do, if it be not their own fault; and *mending their nets* is, in its season, as necessary work as fishing.

5:1 Christ preached this sermon, which was an exposition of the law, upon a mountain, because upon *a mountain* the law was given; and this was also a solemn promulgation of the Christian law. But observe the difference: when *the law was* given, the Lord *came down upon the mountain*; now the Lord *went up*: then, he spoke *in thunder and lightning*; now, *in a still small voice*: then the people were ordered to keep their distance; now they are invited to draw near: a blessed change!

5:19 The Jews reckon the least of the commandments of the law to be that of the bird's nest (Deut. 22:6–7); yet even that had a significance and an intention very great and considerable.

5:22 Anger is a natural passion; there are cases in which it is lawful and laudable; but it is then *sinful*, when we are angry without cause.

5:34 We may be sworn, but we must not swear; we may be adjured, and so obliged to it, but we must not thrust ourselves upon it for our own worldly advantage.

5:38–42 The sum of all is, that Christians must not be litigious; small injuries must be submitted to, and no notice taken of them; and if the injury be such as requires us to seek reparation, it must be for a good end, and without thought of revenge: though we must not invite injuries, yet we must meet them cheerfully in the way of duty, and make the best of them.

5:47 Those who promise themselves a reward above others must study to *do more than others*.

6:3–4 When we take least notice of our good deeds ourselves, God takes most notice of them.

6:7 The danger of this error [much speaking] is when we only *say* our prayers, and not when we *pray* them.

So far is God from being wrought upon by the length or language of our prayers, that the most powerful intercessions are those which are made with *groanings that cannot be uttered*, Rom. 8:26. We are not to *pre*scribe, but *sub*scribe to God.

6:9 He is not only, as a Father, willing to help us, but as a heavenly Father, able to help us, able to do great things for us, more than we can ask or think; he has wherewith to supply our needs, for every good gift is from above. He is a Father, and therefore we may come to him with boldness, but a Father in heaven, and therefore we must come with reverence, Eccles. 5:2.

6:13 The best pleas in prayer are those that are taken from God himself, and from that which he has made known of himself. We must wrestle with God in his own strength, both as to the nature of our pleas and the urging of them.

Praise is the work and happiness of heaven; and all that would go to heaven hereafter, must begin their heaven now.

6:18 Religious fasts, if rightly kept, will shortly be recompensed with an everlasting feast.

6:25 Our *life* is a greater blessing than our *livelihood*.

6:26 You are his children, his first-born; now he that feeds his birds surely will not starve his babes. They trust your Father's providence, and will not you trust it? In dependence upon that, they are careless for the morrow; and being so, they live the merriest lives of all creatures; they *sing among the branches* (Ps. 104:12), and, to the best of their power, they praise their Creator.

6:28 Idleness *tempts* God, instead of *trusting* him; but he that provides for inferior creatures, without their labour, will much more provide for us, by blessing our labour, which he has made our duty. And if we should, through sickness, be unable to *toil* and *spin*, God can furnish us with what is necessary for us.

6:33 O what a blessed change would it make in our hearts and lives, did we but firmly believe this truth, that the best way to be comfortably provided for in this world, is to be most intent upon another world! We then begin at the right end of our work, when we begin with God.

7:1 Because we must not judge others, which is a great sin, it does not therefore follow that we must not reprove others, which is a great duty, and may be a means of *saving a soul from death*; however, it will be a means of saving our souls from sharing in their guilt.

7:11 All the compassions of all the tender fathers in the world ... compared *with the tender mercies of our God*, would be but as a candle to the sun, or a drop to the ocean.

7:22–23 A man may be a preacher, may have gifts for the ministry, and an external call to it, and perhaps some success in it, and yet be a wicked man; may help others to heaven, and yet come short himself. A man might *cast devils out* of others, and yet have a devil, nay, be a devil himself. Gifts of tongues and healing would recommend men to the world, but it is real holiness or sanctification that is accepted of God. Grace will bring a man to heaven without working miracles, but working miracles will never bring a man to heaven without grace.

8:5 The greatest of men must turn beggars, when they have to do with Christ.

8:16–17 Christ bore away sin by the merit of his death, and bore away sickness by the miracles of his life; nay, though those miracles are ceased, we may say, that *he bore our sicknesses* then, *when he bore our sins in his own body upon the tree*; for sin is both the cause and the sting of sickness.

8:25 They who would learn to pray must go to sea. Imminent and sensible dangers will drive people to him who alone can help in time of need.

8:34 There are a great many who prefer their swine before their Saviour, and so come short of Christ, and salvation by him.

9:17 There may be *over*-doing even in *well*-doing, a being *righteous over-much*; and such an *over*-doing as may prove an *un*-doing through the subtlety of Satan.

9:24 Sleep is a short death, and death a long sleep. But *the death of the righteous* is in a special manner to be looked upon as a sleep, Isa. 57:2. They sleep in Jesus (1 Thes. 4:14); they not only rest from the toils and labours of the day, but *rest in hope* of a joyful waking again in the morning of the resurrection.

9:31 Honour is like the shadow, which, as it flees from those that follow it, so it follows those that flee from it.

9:38 The melancholy aspect of the times, and the deplorable state of precious souls, should much excite and quicken prayer. When things look discouraging, we should pray more, and then we should complain and fear less.

10:1 The design of the gospel was to *conquer the devil* and to *cure the world* ... The power that is committed to the ministers of Christ, is directly levelled against the devil and his kingdom ... Moses's miracles were many of them for destruction; those Mahomet pretended to, were for ostentation; but the miracles Christ wrought, and appointed his apostles to work, were all for edification, and evince him to be, not only the great Teacher and Ruler, but the great Redeemer, of the world.

10:28 *Hell* is the destruction both of *soul and body*; not of the *being* of either, but the *well*-being of both; it is the ruin of the whole man; if the soul be lost, the body is lost too.

10:35 The most violent and implacable feuds have ever been those that have arisen from difference in religion; no enmity like that of the persecutors, no resolution like that of the persecuted.

10:37–39 Now thus the terms are settled; if religion be worth *any* thing, it is worth *every* thing: and, therefore, all who believe the truth of it, will soon come up to the price of it; and they who make it their business and bliss, will make everything else to yield to it.

11:1 The increase and multitude of labourers in the Lord's work should not be made an excuse for our negligence, but an encouragement to our diligence. The more busy others are, the more busy we should be, and all little enough, so much work is there to be done.

11:19 The most unspotted innocency, and the most unparalleled excellency, will not always be a fence *against the reproach of tongues.*

11:20 Rough and unpleasing methods must not be taken, till gentler means have first been used. Christ is not *to upbraid; he gives liberally, and upbraideth not*, till sinners by their obstinacy extort it from him. *Wisdom* first invites, but when her invitations are slighted, then she *upbraids*, Prov. 1:20, 24. Those do not go in Christ's method, who begin with upbraidings.

11:22 If self-reproach be the torture of hell, it must needs be hell indeed to those who had such a fair opportunity of getting to heaven.

11:25 Thanksgiving is a proper answer to dark and disquieting thoughts, and may be an effectual means to silence them. Songs of praise are sovereign cordials to drooping souls, and will help to cure melancholy.

11:27 The Father has delivered his all into the hands of the Lord Jesus; let us but deliver our all into his hand and the work is done.

11:29–30 Christ has a *yoke* for our necks, as well as a *crown* for our heads, and this *yoke* he expects we should *take upon* us and draw in. It may be a little hard at first, but it is easy afterwards; the love of God and the hope of heaven will make it *easy.*

11:29 Christ has erected a great school, and has invited us to be his scholars. We must enter ourselves, associate with his scholars, and daily attend the instructions he gives by his word and Spirit. We must *so learn of Christ* as to *learn Christ* (Eph. 4:20), for he is both Teacher and Lesson, Guide and Way, and All in All.

12:1 Hunger is a natural desire which cannot be mortified, but must be gratified, and cannot be put off with anything but meat; therefore we say, It will *break through stone walls.*

13:1–2 Sometimes there is most of the *power* of religion where there is least of the *pomp* of it: *the poor receive the gospel.*

13:3–9 It is a melancholy prospect which this parable gives us of the congregations of those who hear the gospel preached, that scarcely one in four brings forth fruit to perfection. Many are called with the common call, but in few is the eternal choice evidenced by the efficacy of that call, Matt. 20:16.

13:6 Where there is not a principle, though there be a profession, we cannot expect perseverance.

13:7 Prosperity destroys the word in the heart, as much as persecution does; and more dangerously, because more silently: the stones spoiled the root, the thorns spoil the fruit.

13:18 He does not say that this good ground has no stones in it, or no thorns; but there were none that prevailed to hinder its fruitfulness. Saints, in this world, are not perfectly free from the remains of sin; but happily freed from the reign of it.

13:25 Such is the proneness of fallen man to sin, that if the enemy sow the tares, he may even go his way, they will spring up of themselves and do hurt; whereas, when good seed is sown, it must be tended, watered, and fenced, or it will come to nothing.

13:36 It is sad to think how many go away from sermons with the word of grace in their ears, but not the work of grace in their hearts.

13:52 Old experiences, and new observations, all have their use; and we must not content ourselves with old discoveries, but must be adding new.

13:58 Unbelief is the great obstruction to Christ's favours.

14:2 God raises up many faithful ministers out of the ashes of one. There may be the terror of strong convictions, where there is not the truth of a saving conversion.

14:25 He *that made the waters of the sea a wall for the redeemed of the Lord* (Isa. 51:10) here makes them a walk for the Redeemer himself, who, as Lord of all, appears with one foot on the sea and the other on dry land, Rev. 10:2. The same power that made iron to swim (2 Kings 6:6), did this.

14:31 It is the business of faith to resolve doubts, the doubts of sense, in a stormy day, so as even then to keep the head above water.

15:13 What is corrupt, though of God's permitting, is not of his planting; he sows nothing but *good seed in his field*.

15:23 Every accepted prayer is not immediately an answered prayer. Sometimes God seems not to regard his people's prayers ... but it is to prove, and so to *improve*, their faith, and to make his after-appearances for them the more glorious to himself, and the more welcome to them.

15:27 Unbelief is apt to mistake recruits for enemies, and to draw dismal conclusions even from comfortable premises; but faith can find encouragement even in that which is discouraging.

15:28 Because of all graces faith honours Christ most, therefore of all graces Christ honours faith most.

15:31 Miracles, which are the matter of our wonder, must be the matter of our praise; and mercies, which are the matter of our rejoicing, must be the matter of our thanksgiving.

16:2–3 We *know not the balancing of the clouds* (Job 37:16), but we may spell something from the faces of them.

16:13 It is possible for men to have good thoughts of Christ, and yet not right ones, a high opinion of him, and yet not high enough.

16:21 All truths are not to be spoken to all persons at all times, but such as are proper and suitable to their present state.

16:24 Our rule is, not to go a step out of the way of duty, either to meet a cross, or to miss one. We must not by our rashness and indiscretion pull crosses down upon our own heads, but must take them up when they are laid in our way. We must so manage an affliction, that it may not be a stumbling-block or hindrance to us in any service we have to do for God.

17:1 Those that would have a transforming fellowship with God, must not only retire, but ascend; lift up their hearts, and *seek things above*. The call is, *Come up hither*, Rev. 4:1.

17:8 If sometimes we are favoured with special manifestations of divine grace, glimpses and pledges of future glory, yet they are withdrawn presently; two heavens are too much for those to expect that never deserve one.

18:15 It is a good rule, which ordinarily should be observed among Christians, not to speak of our brethren's faults to others, till we have first spoken of them to themselves; this would make less reproaching and more reproving; that is, less sin committed, and more duty done. It will be likely to work upon an offender, when he sees his reprover concerned not only for his salvation, in telling him his fault, but for his reputation in telling him of it privately.

18:18–19 Pass no sentence, which you cannot in faith ask God to confirm.

18:34 Our debts to God are never compounded; either all is forgiven or all is exacted; glorified saints in heaven are pardoned all, through Christ's complete satisfaction; damned sinners in hell are paying all, that is, are punished for all.

19:6 A man's children are pieces of himself, but his wife is himself.

19:8 The law of Moses considered the hardness of men's hearts, but the gospel of Christ cures it; and his grace *takes away the heart of stone, and gives a heart of flesh*. By the law was the knowledge of sin, but by the gospel was the conquest of it.

19:18–19 Though first-table duties have in them more of the essence of religion, yet second-table duties have in them more of the evidence of it. Our light *burns* in love to God, but it *shines* in love to our neighbour.

19:28 Christ's second coming will be a regeneration, when there shall be *new heavens, and a new earth, and the restitution of all things*. All that partake of the regeneration in grace (John 3:3) shall partake of the regeneration in glory; for as grace is the first resurrection (Rev. 20:6), so glory is the second regeneration.

19:29 Now if we could but mix faith with the promise, and trust Christ for the performance of it, surely we should think nothing too much to do, nothing too hard to suffer, nothing too dear to part with, for him.

20:1 The duties of Christianity are more necessary to be known than the notions of it; and yet the notions of it are more necessary to be illustrated than the duties of it; which is that which parables are designed for.

20:22 We know not what we ask, when we ask for the glory of wearing the crown, and ask not for the grace to bear the cross in our way to it. The truth is, Religion, if it be worth any thing, is worth every thing; but it is worth little, if it be not worth suffering for. Now let us sit down, and count the cost of dying for Christ rather than denying him, and ask, Can we take him upon these terms?

20:32 It is the will of God that we should in every thing make our requests known to him by prayer and supplication; not to inform or move him, but to qualify ourselves for the mercy. The waterman in the boat, who with his hook takes hold of the shore, does not thereby pull the shore to the boat, but the boat to the shore. So in prayer we do not draw the mercy to ourselves, but ourselves to the mercy.

21:21 Faith is the soul, prayer is the body; both together make a complete man for any service. Faith, if it be right, will excite prayer; and prayer is not right if it do not spring from faith.

22:15 The more there is of the wicked wit in the contrivance of a sin, the more there is of the wicked will in the commission of it.

22:37–39 Love is the rest and satisfaction of the soul; if we walk in this good old way, we shall find rest.

22:43–45 In expounding scripture we must take notice of, and improve, not only that which is the main scope and sense of a verse, but of the words and phrases, by which the Spirit chooses to express that sense, which have often a very useful and instructive significance. Here is a good note from that word, *My Lord*.

23:37 The chickens naturally run to the hen for shelter, when they are threatened by the birds of prey; perhaps Christ refers to that promise (Ps. 91:4), *He shall cover thee with his feathers.* There is *healing under Christ's wings* (Mal. 4:2); that is more than the hen has for her chickens.

24:15 As Christ by his precepts confirmed the law, so by his predictions he confirmed the prophecies of the Old Testament, and it will be of good use to compare both together.

24:25 Christ's warnings are designed to engage our watchfulness; and though the elect shall be preserved from delusion, yet they shall be preserved by the use of appointed means, and a due regard to the cautions of the word; we are kept through faith, faith in Christ's word, which he has told us before.

24:27 Christ speaks of *shining into the west*, because it spread most effectually into those countries which lay west from Jerusalem, as Mr Herbert observes in his *Church-militant*. How soon did the gospel lightning reach this island of Great Britain. Tertullian, who wrote in the second century, takes notice of it ... —*The fastnesses of Britain, though inaccessible to the Romans, were occupied by Jesus Christ*. This was the Lord's doing.

25:6 Christ will come when he pleases, to show his sovereignty, and will not let us know when, to teach us our duty.

25:20, 22 Our comfort, in the day of account, will be according to our faithfulness, not according to our usefulness; our sincerity, not our success; according to the uprightness of our hearts, not according to the degree of our opportunities.

26:2 Thoughts of a suffering Christ are great supports to a suffering Christian, suffering with him and for him.

26:30 After we have received the Lord's supper, it is good for us to retire for prayer and meditation, and to be alone with God.

26:39 Prayer is never out of season, but it is especially seasonable in an agony.

A prayer of faith against an affliction may very well consist with the patience of hope under affliction.

26:57 The *sheep-gate* was the way into town from the mount of

Olives; and it was so called because the sheep appointed for sacrifice were brought that way to the temple; very fitly therefore is Christ led that way, who is the Lamb of God, that takes away the sin of the world.

27:45 An extraordinary light gave intelligence of the birth of Christ (2:2), and therefore it was proper that an extraordinary darkness should notify his death, for he is the *Light of the world*.

27:46 Christ was made *Sin* for us, a *Curse* for us; and therefore, though God loved him as a Son, he frowned upon him as a Surety.

27:51 Nothing can obstruct or discourage our access to heaven, for the veil is rent; *a door is opened in heaven*, Rev. 4:1.

27:60 It is the most melancholy circumstance in the funerals of our Christian friends, when we have laid their bodies in the dark and silent grave, to go home, and leave them behind; but alas, it is not we that *go home*, and *leave them behind*, no, it is they that are gone to the better home, and have left us behind.

28:7 Public usefulness to others must be preferred before the pleasure of secret communion with God ourselves; for *it is more blessed to give than to receive*.

28:12–13 Here was *large money* given for the advancing of that which they knew to be a lie, yet many grudge a little money for the advancement of that which they know to be the truth, though they have a promise of being reimbursed in the resurrection of the just. Let us never starve a good cause, when we see a bad one so liberally supported.

Mark

1:4 John preached the *remission of sins*, which is the great gospel privilege. He preached *repentance*, in order to it; he told people that there must be a renovation of their hearts and a reformation of their lives, that they must forsake their sins and turn to God, and upon those terms and no other, their sins should be forgiven.

1:16–20 Christ will have followers. If he set up a school, he will have scholars; if he set up his standard, he will have soldiers; if he preach, he will have hearers. He has taken an effectual course to secure this; for *all that the Father has given him, shall*, without fail, *come to him*.

1:35 This *morning* was the morning of the *first day of the week*, which afterward he sanctified, and made remarkable, by another sort of *rising early*.

3:8 *Devils fell down before him* ... and by their own terrors were compelled to own that *he was the Son of God*, v. 11. It is sad that this great truth should be denied by any of the children of men, who may have the benefit of it, when a confession of it has so often been extorted from devils, who are excluded from having benefit by it.

3:14 Christ's ministers must be much with him.

4:1 Methinks Christ's carrying his doctrine into a ship, and preaching it thence, was a presage of his sending the gospel to the *isles of the Gentiles*, and the shipping off of the kingdom of God (that rich cargo) from the Jewish nation, to be sent to a people that would bring forth more of the fruits of it.

4:35 The end of a toil may perhaps be but the beginning of a toss. But observe, the ship that Christ made his pulpit is taken under his special protection, and, though in danger, cannot sink. What is used for Christ, he will take particular care of.

5:24–34 This cure was wrought by *the way*, as he was going to raise the ruler's daughter, and was followed by a crowd. See how Christ improved his time, and lost none of the precious moments of it. Many of his discourses, and some of his miracles, are dated *by the way-side*; we should be doing good, not only when we *sit in the house*, but when we *walk by the way*, Deut. 6:7.

5:36 Keep up a confidence in Christ, and a dependence upon him, and he will do what is for the best. Believe the resurrection, and then be not afraid.

6:12 The great design of gospel preachers, and the great tendency of gospel preaching, should be, to bring people to repentance, to a *new heart* and a *new way*. They did not amuse people with curious speculations, but told them that they must repent of their sins, and turn to God.

6:31 The most active servants of Christ cannot be always upon the stretch of business, but have bodies that require some relaxation, some breathing-time; we shall not be able to serve God without ceasing day and night, till we come to heaven, where they *never rest* from praising him, Rev. 4:8.

6:46 A good man is never less alone than when alone with God.

6:48 The church is often like a ship at sea, *tossed with tempests, and not comforted*; we may have Christ for us, and yet wind and tide against us; but it is a comfort to Christ's disciples in a storm, that their Master is in the heavenly mount, interceding for them.

6:50 When Christ said to those that came to apprehend him by force, *I am he*, they were struck down by it, John 18:6. When he saith to those that come to apprehend him by faith, *I am he*, they are raised up by it, and comforted.

7:21–22 *Ill-thinking* is put first, as that which is the spring of all our *com*missions, and *unthinking* put last, as that which is the spring of all our *o*missions.

8:2 True zeal makes nothing of hardships in the way of duty.

9:5 If it is good to be with Christ transfigured only upon a mountain with Moses and Elias, how good will it be to be with Christ glorified in heaven with all the saints!

9:47 If we be *ruled* by sin, we shall inevitably be *ruined* by it

10:1 In Matthew it is said, *He healed them*; here it is said, *He taught them*: his cures were to confirm his doctrine, and to recommend it, and his doctrine was to explain his cures, and illustrate them.

11:2–7 Christ went upon the water in a *borrowed* boat, ate the Passover in a *borrowed* chamber, was buried in a *borrowed* sepulchre, and here rode on a *borrowed* ass. Let not Christians scorn to be beholden one to another, and, when need is, to go a borrowing, for our Master did not.

12:24 The same power that made soul and body, and preserved them while they were together, can preserve the body safe, and the soul active, when they are parted, and can unite them together again; for *behold the Lord's arm is not shortened*.

12:30 Love is the leading affection of the soul; the love of God is the leading grace in the renewed soul.

12:41–44 Public charities should be encouraged, for they bring upon a nation public blessings; and though there may be some mismanagement of them, yet that is not a good reason why we should not bring in our *quota* to them.

13:7 Those that despise the smiles of the world, and do not court and covet them, may despise the frowns of the world, and need not fear them.

14:24 How comfortable is this to poor repenting sinners, that the blood of Christ is *shed for many*! And if for *many*, why not for *me*? If for sinners, sinners of the Gentiles, the chief of sinners, then *why not for me*?

14:66–72 They that think it dangerous to be in company with Christ's disciples, because thence they may be drawn in to *suffer for him*, will find it much more dangerous to be in company with his enemies, because there they may be drawn in to *sin against him*.

15:17 If we be at any time afflicted with a *thorn in the flesh*, let it be our comfort, that our high priest is touched with the feeling of our infirmities, having himself known what *thorns in the flesh* meant.

15:26 Whenever we look unto Christ crucified, we must remember the inscription over his head, that he is a king, and we must give up ourselves to be his subjects, as Israelites indeed.

15:42 Such work is to be done, and such advantages are to be gained on the sabbath day, that it is requisite we should get ready for it a day before; nay, the whole week should be divided between the improvement of the foregoing sabbath and the preparation for the following sabbath.

15:46 When Daniel was put into the lions' den, a stone was laid to the mouth of it to keep him in, as here to the door of Christ's sepulchre, but neither of them could keep off the angels' visits to the prisoners.

16:3 They who are carried by a holy zeal, to seek Christ diligently, will find the difficulties that lie in their way strangely to vanish, and themselves helped over them beyond their expectation.

16:6 As angels rejoice in the conversion of sinners, so they do also in the consolation of saints.

Luke

1:37 No word of God must be incredible to us, as long as no work of God is impossible to him.

1:39–40 Sometimes it may prove a better piece of service than we think to bring good people together, to compare notes.

It is very beneficial and comfortable for those that have a good work of grace begun in their souls, and Christ in the forming there, to consult those who are in the same case, that they may communicate experiences one to another; and they will find that, as in water face answers to face, so doth the heart of man to man, of Christian to Christian.

1:63 When ministers have their mouths stopped, that they cannot preach, yet they may be doing good as long as they have not their hands tied, that they cannot write.

2:9 We are not out of the way of divine visits when we are sensibly employed in an honest calling, and abide with God in it.

2:19 The truths of Christ are worth keeping; and the way to keep them safe is to ponder them. Meditation is the best help to memory.

2:29 See here, how comfortable the death of a good man is; he departs as God's servant from the place of his toil to that of his rest. He departs in peace, peace with God, peace with his own conscience; in peace with death, well-reconciled to it, well-acquainted with it.

2:52 Young people, as they grow in stature, should grow in wisdom, and then, as they grow in wisdom, they will grow in favour with God and man.

3:3 The design of the gospel, which now began, was to make men devout and pious, holy and heavenly, humble and meek, sober and chaste, just and honest, charitable and kind, and good in every relation, who had been much otherwise; and this is to repent.

3:16 John was a prophet, yea more than a prophet, more so than any of the Old-Testament prophets; but Christ was a prophet more than John, for it was both by the Spirit of Christ, and of the grace of Christ, that all the prophets prophesied, and John among the rest, 1 Peter 1:10–11.

3:21 The inward and spiritual grace of which sacraments are the outward and visible signs must be fetched in by prayer; and therefore prayer must always accompany them.

When he [Jesus] prayed, the heaven was opened. He that by his power parted the waters, to make a way through them to Canaan, now by his power parted the air, another fluid element, to open a correspondence with the heavenly Canaan. Thus was there opened to Christ, and by him to us, a new and living way into the holiest; sin had shut up heaven, but Christ's prayer opened it again. Prayer is an ordinance that opens heaven: Knock, and it shall be opened unto you.

4:1–2 When we have had the most comfortable communion with God, and the clearest discoveries of his favour to us, we may expect that Satan will set upon us (the richest ship is the pirate's prize), and that God will suffer him to do so, that the power of his grace may be manifested and magnified.

4:4 *It is written.* This is the first word recorded as spoken by Christ after his instalment in his prophetical office … The word of God is our *sword*, and faith in that word is our *shield*; we should therefore be *mighty in the scriptures*, and go *in that might*, go forth and go on, in our spiritual warfare, know *what is written*, for it is *for our learning*, for *our use*.

4:9–11 It is true, God has promised the protection of angels, to encourage us to trust him, not to tempt him; as far as the promise of God's presence with us, so far the promise of the angels' ministration goes, but no further: 'They shall keep thee when thou goest on the ground, where thy way lies, but not if thou wilt presume to fly in the air.'

4:40 The sign he used in healing was *laying his hands* on the sick; not lifting up his hands for them, for he healed as having authority. He healed by his own power. And thus he would put honour upon that sign which was afterwards used in conferring the Holy Ghost.

5:4 We must not abruptly quit the callings wherein we are called because we have not the success in them we promised ourselves. The ministers of the gospel must continue to *let down that net*, though they have perhaps *toiled long* and *caught nothing*; and this is thank-worthy, to continue unwearied in our labours, though we see not the success of them.

6:13 In serving God, our great care should be, not to *lose time*, but to make the end of one good duty the beginning of another.

6:24 It is the *folly* of carnal worldlings that they make the things of this world *their consolation*, which were intended only for their *convenience*.

6:40 Christ's followers cannot expect better treatment in the world than their Master had.

7:3 We may now, by faithful and fervent prayer, apply ourselves to Christ in heaven, and ought to do so, when sickness is in our families; for Christ is still the great Physician.

7:4 Building places of meeting for religious worship is a very *good work*, is an instance of love to God and his people; and those who do good works of that kind are *worthy of double honour*.

7:33–34 It appears that the ministers of Christ may be of very different tempers and dispositions, very different ways of preaching and living, and yet all good and useful; *diversity of gifts*, but each given to *profit withal*.

8:10 Happy are we, and for ever indebted to free grace, if the same thing that is a *parable* to others, with which they are only *amused*, is a *plain truth* to us, by which we are *enlightened* and *governed*, and into the mould of which we are *delivered*.

8:22 They that observe Christ's orders may assure themselves of his presence. If Christ sends his disciples, he goes *with them*. And those may safely and boldly venture any where that have Christ accompanying them.

8:24 Thus Christ showed that, though the devil pretends to be the prince of the power of the air, yet even there he has him in a chain.

9:11 Christ still has a power over bodily diseases, and heals his people that *need healing*. Sometimes he sees that we need the *sickness* for the good of our souls, more than the *healing* for the ease of our bodies, and then we must be willing *for a season*, because *there is need*, to be in *heaviness*; but, when he sees that we *need healing*, we shall have it.

9:28–29 He [Christ] intended to put an *honour* upon the duty of prayer, and to *recommend* it to us. It is a transfiguring, transforming duty; if our hearts be elevated and enlarged in it, so as in it to *behold the glory of the Lord*, we shall be *changed into the same image from glory to glory*, 2 Cor. 3:18. By prayer we fetch in the wisdom, grace and joy, which *make the face to shine*.

9:51 All good Christians may frame to themselves the same notion of death, and may call it their being *received up*, to be with Christ where he is; and, when the *time* of their being *received up* is at hand, let them lift up their heads, knowing that *their redemption draws nigh*.

10:17 Whatever advantages we gain, he must have all the praise; if the work be done *in* his name, the honour is due *to* his name.

10:20 Saving graces are more to be rejoiced in than spiritual gifts; holy love is *a more excellent way* than speaking with tongues.

10:34 A great mercy it is to have inns upon the road, where we may be furnished for our money with all conveniences for food and rest.

10:39 A good sermon is never the worse for being preached in a house; and the visits of our friends should be so managed as to make them turn to a spiritual advantage.

10:40 It does not become the disciples of Christ to affect *much serving*, to affect varieties, dainties and superfluities in eating and drinking; what need is there of *much serving*, when much less will serve?

11:1 Prayer is one of the great laws of natural religion. That man is a brute, is a monster, that never prays, that never gives glory to his Maker, nor feels his favour, nor owns his dependence upon him.

12:2 The day is coming when hypocrites will be stripped of their fig-leaves.

12:6–7 Now a firm belief of the doctrine of God's universal providence, and the extent of it, will be satisfying to us when at any time we are in peril, and will encourage us to trust God in the way of duty.

12:15 The things of the world will not suit the nature of a soul, nor supply its needs, nor satisfy its desires, nor last so long as it will last.

12:17 Disquieting care is the common fruit of an abundance of this world, and the common fault of those that have abundance.

12:21 It is the unspeakable folly of the most of men to mind and pursue the wealth of this world more than the wealth of the other world, that which is merely for the body and for time, more than that which is for the soul and eternity.

12:59 Christ's sufferings were short, yet the *value* of them made them fully satisfactory. In the sufferings of damned sinners, what is wanting in value must be made up in an endless duration.

13:11 Even bodily infirmities, unless they be very grievous indeed, should not keep us from public worship on sabbath days; for God can help us, beyond our expectation.

13:24 The reason why many come short of grace and glory is because they rest in a *lazy seeking* of that which will not be attained without a *laborious striving*.

13:27 Under a pretence of piety, they kept up secret haunts of sin, and did the devil's drudgery in Christ's livery.

15:14 Wilful waste brings woeful want.

16:16 Those that would go to heaven must take pains, must strive against the stream, must press against the crowd that are going the contrary way.

16:22 Saints die, that they may bring their sorrows to an end, and may enter upon their joys. Sinners die, that they may go to give up their account. It concerns both rich and poor to prepare for death, for it waits for them both.

19:17 They who do that which is good shall have *praise of the same*. *Do well*, and Christ will say to thee, *Well done*; and, if he says *Well done*, the matter is not great who says otherwise.

19:19 There are *degrees of glory* in heaven; every vessel will be alike *full*, but not alike *large*. And the degrees of glory there will be according to the degrees of usefulness here.

19:48 Till his hour was come his interest in the common people protected him; but, when his hour was come, the chief priests' influence upon the common people delivered him up.

20:9 Whereas man was, for sin, condemned to *till the ground*, they that have a place in the church are restored to that which was Adam's work in innocency, to *dress the garden*, and to keep it; for the church is a paradise, and Christ the tree of life in it.

21:19 In difficult times, when we can keep possession of nothing else, then let us make that sure which may be made sure, and keep possession of our souls. It is by patience, Christian patience, that we keep possession of our own souls.

21:36 Those shall be accounted worthy to live a life of praise in the other world that live a life of prayer in this world. A great part of our worthiness lies in an acknowledgment of our own unworthiness.

22:15 Our gospel Passover, eaten by faith with Jesus Christ, will be an excellent preparation for sufferings, and trials, and death itself.

22:20 Had it not been for the blood of Christ, we had never had the New Testament; and, had it not been for the New Testament, we had never known the meaning of Christ's blood shed.

22:46 When we find ourselves either by our outward circumstances or our inward dispositions entering into temptation, it concerns us to *rise and pray*, Lord, help me in this *time of need*.

23:40–43 Though it is certain that true repentance is never too late, it is as certain that late repentance is seldom true.

23:42 He went by the cross to the crown, and we must not think of going any other way, or of being perfected but by sufferings.

23:46 Christ died with scripture in his mouth. Thus he directs us to make use of scripture language in our addresses to God. We must show that we are freely willing to die, that we firmly believe in another life after this, and are desirous of it by saying, *Father, into thy hands I commend my spirit.*

24:12 Many that are *swift-footed* enough when there is no danger are but *cow-hearted* when there is.

24:30 Whenever we *sit down to eat*, let us set Christ at the upper end of the table, take our meat as *blessed to us* by him, and *eat and drink* to his glory, and receive contentedly and thankfully what he is pleased to *carve* out to us, be the fare ever so coarse and mean. We may well receive it cheerfully, if we can by faith see it coming to us *from* Christ's hand, and with his blessing.

24:36 He had promised that after his resurrection he *would see them in Galilee*; but so desirous was he to see them, and satisfy them, that he anticipated the appointment and *sees them at Jerusalem*. Christ is often *better* than his word, but never *worse*.

24:45 In his discourse with the two disciples he took the veil from off the text, by *opening* the scriptures; here he took the veil from off the heart *by opening the mind*.

John to Acts

John

1:10 He left a world of bliss and glory, and was here in this melancholy miserable world.

1:25 Divine justice drowned the old world *in its filth*, but divine grace has provided for the cleansing of this new world *from its filth*.

1:34 God's children are made manifest by their *graces*; their glories are reserved for their future state.

2:2 It is the wisdom of the prudent to study how to *improve* conversation rather than how to *decline* it.

2:4 The delays of mercy are not to be construed the denials of prayer. *At the end it shall speak.*

3:36 Grace is glory begun.

4:1 The success of the gospel exasperates its enemies, and it is a good sign that it is getting ground when the powers of darkness are enraged against it.

4:11 There are those who will trust Christ no further than they can see him, and will not believe his promise, unless the means of the performance of it be *visible*; as if he were tied to our methods, and could not draw water without our buckets.

5:19 *God cannot* lie, *cannot deny* himself, which expresses the perfection of his truth, not any imperfection in his strength.

6:18 The ship of the church, in which the disciples of Christ have *embarked* themselves and their all, may be much shattered and distressed, yet it shall come safe to the harbour at last: *tossed* at sea, but not *lost*.

6:26 Many follow Christ for *loaves*, and not for *love*.

6:27 Everlasting life—we are told to *labour for it*, as if it were to be got by our own industry … but the Son of man *gives it*.

6:70–71 Hypocrites and betrayers of Christ are no better than devils.

7:1 Gospel light is justly *taken away* from those that endeavour to extinguish it.

In times of imminent peril it is not only *allowable*, but *advisable*, to *withdraw* and *abscond* for our own safety and preservation, and to choose the service of those places which are least perilous (Matt. 10:23).

8:21 Unbelief is the damning sin; it is a sin against the remedy.

8:42 All that have God for their Father have a true love to Jesus Christ, and esteem of his person, a grateful sense of his love, a sincere affection to his cause and kingdom, a complacency in the salvation wrought out by him and in the method and terms of it, and a care to keep his commandments, which is the surest evidence of our love to him.

8:56 No joy like the joy of faith; we are never acquainted with true pleasure till we are acquainted with Christ.

8:57 Old age is reckoned to begin at fifty (Num. 4:47).

9:3 The sentences in the book of providence are sometimes *long*, and you must read a great way before you can apprehend the sense of them.

9:4 Whom God sends he employs, for he sends none to be idle.

The consideration of our death approaching should quicken us to improve all the opportunities of life, both for doing and getting good.

9:5 What were candles made for but to burn?

9:21 This implies that while children are not of age (while they are *infants*, such as cannot speak), it is incumbent upon their parents to *speak for them*, speak to God for them in prayer, speak to the church for them in baptism; but when they are of age, it is fit that they should be asked whether they be willing to stand to that which their parents did for them, and let them speak for themselves.

9:31–33 'See here,' saith Dr Whitby, 'a blind man and unlearned judging more rightly of divine things than the whole learned council of the Pharisees, whence we learn that we are not always to be led by the authority of councils, popes or bishops; and that it is not absurd for laymen sometimes to vary from their opinions, these overseers being sometimes guilty of great oversights.'

10:33 God himself is out of the sinner's reach, and not capable of receiving any real injury; and therefore enmity to God spits its venom at his name, and so shows its ill-will.

11:3 Our love to him is not worth speaking of, but his to us can never be enough spoken of.

11:4 The body's death to this world is the soul's birth into another world.

11:7 Christ never brings his people into any peril but he accompanies them in it, and is with them even when they *walk through the valley of the shadow of death*.

11:11 Death itself does not break the bond of friendship between Christ and a believer. Lazarus is dead, and yet he is still *our friend*.

11:16 How pleasantly does the good man speak of dying, as if it were but undressing and going to bed!

11:23 It is a matter of comfort to us, when we have buried our godly friends and relations, to think that they shall *rise again*.

As bone shall return to his bone in that day, so friend to his friend.

It is an unspeakable comfort to all good Christians that Jesus Christ is the resurrection and the life, and will be so to them.

11:25–27 The crosses and comforts of this present time would not make such an impression upon us as they do if we did but believe the things of eternity as we ought.

11:27 *Even so*. Faith is an echo to divine revelation, returns the same words, and resolves to abide by them: *Yea Lord, As the word did make it so I believe and take it*, said queen Elizabeth.

11:28 Mr George Herbert took pleasure in calling Christ, *my Master*.

11:36 Though our tears profit not the dead, they embalm their memory.

11:51 Words of prophecy in the mouth are no infallible evidence of a principle of grace in the heart.

12:32–33 The cross of Christ, though to some a *stumbling-stone*, is to others a *loadstone*.

12:34 We have heard out of the gospel that which exalts free grace, we have heard also that which enjoins duty, and we must cordially embrace both, and not separate them, nor set them at variance.

12:47 Though he had authority to judge, he suspended the execution of it, because he had work of another nature to do first, and that was to *save the world*.

12:48 Those shall not be condemned for their infidelity that never had, nor could have, the gospel; every man shall be judged according to the dispensation of light he was under: *Those that have sinned without law shall be judged without law*. But those that have heard, or might have heard, and would not, lie open to this doom.

13:3–4 A well-grounded assurance of heaven and happiness, instead of puffing a man up with pride, will make and keep him very humble.

13:35 Brotherly love is the badge of Christ's disciples. By this he knows them, by this they may know themselves (1 John 2:14), and by this others may know them.

14:1 The joy of faith is the best remedy against the griefs of sense.

14:3 As the resurrection of Christ is the assurance of our resurrection, so his ascension, victory, and glory, are an assurance of ours.

14:15–17 Follow the conduct of the Spirit, and you shall have the comfort of the Spirit.

14:23 Love is the root, obedience is the fruit.

15:20 The plainest truths are sometimes the strongest arguments for the hardest duties.

16:13 We should not grudge that the Spirit does not now *show us things to come* in this world, as he did to the apostles; let it suffice that the Spirit in the word hath *shown us things to come* in the other world, which are our chief concern.

16:16 The most that death does to our Christian friends is to take them out of our sight, not out of being, not out of bliss, not out of all relation to us, only out of sight, and then not out of mind.

16:22 When the sun sets, the sun-flower will hang the head. And Christ takes notice of these griefs, has a bottle for the tears, and a book for the sighs, of all gracious mourners.

16:28 The principles of the oracles of God brought into a little compass in creeds and catechisms have, like the beams of the sun contracted in a burning glass, conveyed divine light and heat with a wonderful power.

16:29 Observe how they triumphed, as the mathematician did with his eureka, eureka, when he had hit upon a demonstration he had long been in quest of: *I have found it, I have found it.* Note, When Christ is pleased to speak plainly to our souls, and to bring us with open face to behold his glory, we have reason to rejoice in it.

16:32 Those that converse with God in solitude are never less alone than when alone. A good God and a good heart are good company at any time.

17:2–3 Grace in the soul is heaven in that soul.

17:3 Those that are acquainted with God and Christ are already in the suburbs of life eternal.

17:5 Promises are not designed to supersede prayers, but to be the guide of our desires and the ground of our hopes.

17:6 *Thine they were.* The elect, whom the father gave to Christ, were his own in three ways: *First*, They were creatures; *Secondly*, They were criminals; *Thirdly*, They were chosen, and their lives and beings were designed, for him; they were set apart for God, and were consigned to Christ as his agent.

18:1 Christ's sufferings began in a garden. In the Garden of Eden sin began; there the curse was pronounced, there the Redeemer was promised, and therefore in a garden that promised seed entered the lists with the old serpent.

19:16 Christ was *made sin for us.* We deserved to have been condemned, but Christ was condemned for us, that to us there might be *no condemnation.* God was now entering into judgment with his Son, that he might not enter into judgment with his servants.

19:18 And now let us pause awhile, and with an eye of faith look upon Jesus. Was ever sorrow like unto his sorrow? See him who was clothed with glory stripped of it all, and clothed with shame—him who was *the praise of angels* made a *reproach of men*—him who had been with eternal delight and joy in the bosom of his Father now in the extremities of pain and agony. See him bleeding, see him struggling, see him dying, see him and love him, love him and live to him, and study what we shall render.

19:32 The extremity of dying agonies is no obstruction to the living comforts that wait for holy souls on the other side of death.

19:34 It is not the water in the font that will be to us *the washing of regeneration*, but the water out of the side of Christ; not the blood of the grape that will pacify the conscience and refresh the soul, but the blood out of the side of Christ.

20:21 Christ had left them his peace for their legacy (14:27). By the death of the testator the testament was become of force, and he was now risen from the dead, to prove the will, and to be himself the executor of it. Accordingly, he here makes prompt payment of the legacy: *Peace be unto you.*

20:25 Christ had chosen them to be his witnesses of this very thing to all nations; and yet Thomas, one of their own fraternity, would not allow them to be competent witnesses, nor trust them further than he could see them.

20:26 Christ did not appear to Thomas, for his satisfaction, till he found him in society with the rest of his disciples, because he would countenance the meetings of Christians and ministers, for there will he be *in the midst of them.*

21:6 The draught of fishes may be considered, (1.) As a miracle in itself. (2.) As a mercy to them. (3.) As the memorial of a former mercy. (4.) As a mystery, and very significant of that work to which Christ was now with an enlarged commission sending them forth.

21:13 The entertainment here was but ordinary ... plain and homely. Hunger is the best sauce.

21:15 The great thing Christ eyes in penitents is their eyeing him in their repentance.

Acts

1:4 Christ thought the promise of the Spirit a legacy worth leaving to his church.

1:7 Vain curiosity is a corrupt humour, to be mortified, and not gratified.

1:14 *They continued in prayer and supplication;* for as praise for the promise is a decent way of begging for the performance, and praise for former mercy of begging further mercy, so, in seeking to God, we give him the glory of the mercy and grace which we have found in him.

2:1 This feast of Pentecost happened on the *first day of the week*, which was an additional honour put on that day, and a confirmation of it to be the Christian Sabbath, *the day which the Lord hath made*, to be a standing memorial in his church of those two great blessings—the resurrection of Christ, and the pouring out of the Spirit, both on that day of the week ... every Lord's day in the year, I think, there should be a full and particular notice taken in our prayers and praises of these two, as there is by some churches of the one once a year, upon Easter-day, and of the other once a year, upon Whit-Sunday. Oh! That we may do it with suitable affections!

2:4 Archbishop Tillotson thinks it probable that if the conversion of infidels to Christianity were now sincerely and vigorously attempted, by men of honest minds, God would extraordinarily countenance such an attempt with all fitting assistance, as he did the first publication of the gospel.

3:2 Those that need, and cannot work, must not be ashamed to beg. Our prayers and our alms should go together. It is a pity that common beggars at church doors should any of them be of such character as to discourage charity; but they ought not always to be overlooked: some there are surely that merit regard, and better feed ten drones, yea, and some wasps, than let one bee starve.

4:32 They did not say that aught was their own; for we can call nothing our own but sin.

9:6 Those whom God will employ are first struck with a sense of their unworthiness to be employed.

9:26 *They believed not that he was a disciple.* There is need of the wisdom of the serpent, to keep the mean between the extremes of suspicion on the one hand and credulity on the other; yet methinks it is safer to err on the charitable side, because it is an adjudged case that it is better the tares should be found among the wheat than that the wheat should any of it be rooted up and thrown out of the field.

10:1–2 Goodness makes greatness truly valuable, and greatness makes goodness much more serviceable.

The gospel has that in it which may recommend it to men of polite learning and a liberal education.

11:18 Wherever God designs to give life he gives repentance; for this is a necessary preparative for the comforts of a sealed pardon and a settled peace in this world, and for the seeing and enjoying of God in the other world.

11:23 To cleave to the Lord Jesus is to live a life of dependence upon him and devotedness to him: not only to hold him fast, but to hold fast by him, to *be strong in the Lord and in the power of his might*.

12:10 Miracles are not to be expected when ordinary means are to be used.

12:11 But *when the Comforter comes*, *whom the Father will send* sooner or later, he will let them know of a surety what a blessed change is wrought in them, and what a happy state they are brought into.

12:12 God's providence leaves room for the use of our prudence; and, though he has undertaken to perform and perfect what he has begun, yet he expects we should consider the thing.

12:23 Surprising discoveries have of late been made by microscopes of the multitude of worms that there are in human bodies, and how much they contribute to the diseases of them, which is a good reason why we should not be proud of our bodies, or of any of their accomplishments, and why we should not pamper our bodies, for this is but feeding the worms, and feeding them for the worms.

12:25 Educating young men for the ministry, and entering them into it, is a very good work for elder ministers to take care of, and of good service to the rising generation.

13:1 Prophets we are not now any longer to expect.

13:47 This prophecy has had its accomplishment in part in the setting up of the kingdom of Christ in this island of ours, which lies, as it were, in the *ends of the earth*, a corner of the world, and shall be accomplished more and more when the time comes for the *bringing in of the fullness of the Gentiles*.

14:27 God's grace can do any thing without ministers' preaching; but ministers' preaching, even Paul's, can do nothing without God's grace.

15:9 We ought not to make any conditions of our brethren's acceptance with us but such as God has made the conditions of their acceptance with him.

15:12 As in natural philosophy and medicine nothing is so satisfactory as experiments, and in law nothing is so satisfactory as cases adjudged, so in the things of God the best explication of the word of grace is the accounts given of the operations of the Spirit of grace.

15:41 Ministers are well employed, and ought to think themselves so, and be satisfied, when they are made use of in confirming those that believe, as well as in converting those that believe not.

16:14 Hearing the word of God is a part of religious worship, and how can we expect God should hear our prayers if we will not hearken to his word?

When a sinner is effectually persuaded to embrace Christ, *then the heart is opened for the King of glory to come in*—the understanding is opened to receive the divine light, the will opened to receive the divine law, and the affections opened to receive the divine love.

17:28 Human learning is both ornamental and serviceable to a gospel minister, especially for the convincing of those that are without; for it enables him to beat them at their own weapons, and to cut off Goliath's head with his own sword.

18:11 Ministers may be serving Christ, and promoting the ends of their ministry, by writing good letters, as well as by preaching good sermons.

19:31 We may be called to lay down our lives, but not to throw away our lives.

20:20 Ministers should, in their private visits, and as they go from house to house, discourse of those things which they have taught publicly, repeat them, inculcate them, and explain them, if it be needful, asking, *Have you understood all these things?*

20:24 Those that have their conversation in heaven can look down, not only upon the common troubles of this earth but upon the threatening rage and malice of hell itself, and say that none of these things moved them.

We have our labours appointed us, for we were not sent into the world to be idle.

We must look upon it as the business of our life to provide for a joyful death, that we may not only die safely, but die comfortably.

20:36 Public prayers are so far from being intended to supersede our own secret prayers, and make them needless, that they are designed to quicken and encourage them, and to direct us in them. When we are alone we should pray over the prayers that our ministers have put up with us.

20:38 When our friends are separated from us by death, this is the consideration with which we raise up our mourning, that we shall see their faces no more; but we complain not of this as those that have no hope, for if our friends died in Christ, and we live to him, they are gone to see God's face, to behold his glory, with the reflection of which their faces shine, and we hope to be with them shortly. Though we shall see their faces no more in this world, we hope to see them again in a better world, and to be there together for ever and with the Lord.

21:16 It is an honourable thing to be an old disciple of Jesus Christ, to have been enabled by the grace of God to continue long in the course of duty, steadfast in the faith, and growing more and more prudent and experienced to a good old age. And with these old disciples one would choose to lodge; for the multitude of their years will teach wisdom.

24:16 Conscience is God's deputy in my soul.

24:26 I ought not to bribe a man to do an unjust thing, but, if he will not do me justice without a fee, it is but doing myself justice to give it to him; and, if they might do it, it was a shame they did not do it. I blush for them, that they would let such an eminent and useful man as Paul lie in the jail, when a little money would have fetched him out, and restored him to his usefulness again.

25:11 Not that all who have committed any thing worthy of death are obliged to accuse themselves, and offer themselves to justice; but, when they are accused and brought to justice, they ought to submit, and to say both God and the government are righteous; as it is necessary that some should be made examples.

26:20 Those that profess repentance must practise it, must live a life of repentance, must in every thing carry it as becomes penitents. It is not enough to speak penitent words, but we must do works agreeable to those words. As true faith, so true repentance, will work.

26:24 The apostles, who were fishermen, were despised because they had no learning; Paul, who was a university-man, and bred a Pharisee, is despised as having too much learning, more than did him good.

Volume 8

Romans to Revelation

Romans

1:16 I reckon him a Christian indeed that is neither ashamed of the gospel nor a shame to it.

1:17 The faith that justifies us is no less than our taking Christ for our Saviour, and becoming true Christians, according to the tenor of the baptismal covenant. There is faith justifying us; there is faith maintaining us; and so *there is righteousness from faith to faith*. Faith is all in all, both in the beginning and progress of a Christian life.

2:15 Conscience is that candle of the Lord which was not quite put out, no, not in the Gentile world. The heathen have witnessed to the comfort of a good conscience.

2:20 Those whose knowledge rests in an empty notion, and does not make an impression on their hearts, have only the form of it, like a picture well drawn and in good colours, but which wants life.

3:2 The enjoyment of God's word and ordinances is the chief happiness of a people.

4:20 Unbelief is at the bottom of all our staggerings at God's promises.

5:9 It is the wrath of God that is the fire of hell.

Christ dying was the testator who bequeathed us the legacy; but Christ living is the executor, who pays it.

5:11 Receiving the atonement is our actual reconciliation to God in justification, grounded upon Christ's satisfaction.

5:14 Original sin is a want of conformity to, and actual sin is a transgression of, the law of God: therefore all were under some law. His proof of it is, *Death reigned from Adam to Moses*.

5:16–17 The stream of grace and righteousness is deeper and broader than the stream of guilt; for this righteousness does not only take away the guilt of that one offence, but of many other offences, even of all.

5:18–21 Surely Adam could not propagate so strong a poison but Jesus Christ could propagate as strong an antidote, and much stronger.

6:4 Before, self was the chief and highest end, but now God. To live indeed is to live to God, with our eyes ever towards him, making him the centre of all our actions.

6:12 It was sin that made our bodies mortal, and therefore do not yield obedience to such an enemy.

6:23 Death is as due to a sinner when he hath sinned as wages are to a servant when he hath done his work.

8:3–4 It was great condescension that he who was God should be made in the likeness of flesh; but much greater that he who was holy should be made in the likeness of sinful flesh.

8:5 The man is as the mind is.

8:6 Spiritual-mindedness is eternal life and peace begun, and an assuring earnest of the perfection of it.

8:21 The fire at the last day shall be a refining, not a destroying annihilating fire. What becomes of the souls of brutes, that go downwards, none can tell. But it should seem by the scripture that there will be some kind of restoration to them. And if it be objected, What use will they be of to glorified saints? We may suppose them of as much use as they were to Adam in innocency; and if it be only to illustrate the wisdom, power and goodness of their Creator, that is enough.

8:23 The children of God have bodies as well as souls; and till those bodies are brought into the glorious liberty of the children of God, the adoption is not perfect.

8:28 Either directly or indirectly, every providence has a tendency to the spiritual good of those that love God, breaking them off from sin, bringing them nearer to God, weaning them from the world, fitting them for heaven.

9:1–2 Dip the nail in oil, it will drive the better.

9:8 It was through faith that Isaac was conceived (Heb. 11:11). Thus were the great mysteries of salvation taught under the Old Testament, not in express words, but by significant types and dispensations of providence, which to them then were not so clear as they are to us now, when the veil is taken away, and the types are expounded by the antitypes.

9:18 Herein the work of our salvation is admirably well ordered that those who are saved must thank God only, and those who perish must thank themselves only (Hosea 13:9). The drawing of souls in order to that coming is a preventing distinguishing favour to whom he will.

9:19 We can destroy ourselves fast enough, but we cannot save ourselves. Sinners fit themselves for hell, but it is God that prepares saints for heaven.

10:1 There may be desires in the heart and yet no prayer, unless those desires be presented to God. Wishing and woulding, if that be all, are not praying.

10:4 The moral law was but for the searching of the wound, the ceremonial law for the shadowing forth of the remedy; but Christ is the end of both.

11:6 Faith has a peculiar fitness to receive the free grace of God for our justification, but not to receive that grace for our election.

11:17 Men graft to mend the tree; but God grafts to mend the branch. The church of God is an olive-tree. Those that are out of the church are as wild olive-trees. Conversion is the grafting in of wild branches. Those that are grafted into the good olive-tree partake of the root and fatness of the olive ... it is applicable to a saving union with Christ.

13:10 Loving and being loved is all the pleasure, joy, and happiness, of an intelligent being.

13:14 By baptism we have in profession put on Christ (Gal. 3:27).

14:4 In judging and censuring our brethren, we meddle with that which does not belong to us: we have work enough to do at home; and, if we must needs be judging, let us exercise our faculty upon our own hearts and ways.

14:7–8 The business of our lives is not to please ourselves, but to please God.

14:17 Nothing is more destructive to true Christianity than placing it in modes, and forms, and circumstantials, which eat out the essentials.

15:5 The more patience and comfort we receive from God, the better disposed we are to love one another. Nothing breaks the peace more than an impatient, and peevish and fretful melancholy temper.

15:12 Christ, as God, was David's root; Christ, as man, was David's offspring.

Faith is the soul's confidence in Christ and dependence on him.

15:20 Commonly the greatest success of the gospel is at its first coming to a place; afterwards people become sermon-proof.

15:23–24, 29 It is wisdom for every one of us to order our affairs so that we may do the most work in the least time.

15:26 They thus extended their bounty and liberality to them, to teach us as we have ability, to stretch out the hand of our charity to all that are of the household of faith, though in places distant from us. Yet, sometimes when more public instances of poverty are presented as objects of our charity, though a great way off from us, we must extend our bounty, as the sun his beams.

16:18 It is an easy thing to be godly from the teeth outward.

16:26 The gospel is revealed, not to be talked of and disputed about, but to be submitted to.

16:27 In thanking God, we fasten upon his favours to us; in praising and adoring God, we fasten upon his perfections in himself.

1 Corinthians

1:10 In the great things of religion be of a mind: but, when there is not a unity of sentiment, let there be a union of affections.

2:2 Christ, in his person and offices, is the sum and substance of the gospel, and ought to be the great subject of a gospel minister's preaching.

2:10–11 The Spirit of God knows the things of God because he is one with God.

5:7–8 Love is the very essence and life of the Christian religion.

6:18 Other vices may be conquered in fight, this only by flight.

11:1 Ministers are likely to preach most to the purpose when they can press their hearers to follow their example.

12:13 Christians become members of this body by baptism. The outward rite is of divine institution, significant of the new birth, called therefore *the washing of regeneration* (Titus 3:5). But it is by the Spirit, by the renewing of the Holy Ghost, that we are made members of Christ's body.

12:17–18 Variety in the members of the body contributes to the beauty of it. We should be doing the duties of our own place, and not murmuring in ourselves, nor quarrelling with others, that we are not in theirs.

12:26 Christian sympathy is a great branch of Christian duty.

12:29–30 How blessed a constitution were the Christian church, if all the members did their duty!

12:31 To have the heart glow with mutual love is vastly better than to glare with the most pompous titles, offices or powers.

13:4 If we love our neighbour we shall be so far from envying his welfare, or being displeased with it, that we shall share in it and rejoice at it. The prosperity of those to whom we wish well can never grieve us; and the mind which is bent on doing good to all can never wish ill to any.

13:12 Now we can only discern things at a great distance, as through a telescope, and that involved in clouds and obscurity; but hereafter the things to be known will be near and obvious, open to our eyes.

15:58 Those who serve God have good wages; they cannot do too much for so good a Master. If they serve him now, they shall see him hereafter; if they suffer for him on earth, they shall reign with him in heaven; if they die for his sake, they shall rise again from the dead, be crowned with glory, honour and immortality, and inherit eternal life.

16:19 Every Christian family should in some respects be a Christian church. In some cases (as, for instance, were they cast away on a foreign shore, where there are no other Christians), they should be a church themselves, if large enough, and live in the use of all ordinances.

2 Corinthians

1:8 Our extremity is God's opportunity.

1:22 The illumination of the Spirit is an earnest of everlasting light; and the comforts of the Spirit are an earnest of everlasting joy.

5:6, 8 True Christians ... should take courage, when encountering the last enemy, and be willing rather to die than live, when it is the will of God that they should *put off this tabernacle*. We shall ... close our eyes to all things in this world, and open them in a world of glory. Faith will be turned into sight.

5:16 Those who make images of Christ, and use them in their worship, do not take the way that Christ has appointed for strengthening their faith and quickening their affections; for it is the will of God that we should not know Christ any more after the flesh.

Galatians

1:20 A solemn oath ... will not justify us in solemn appeals to God upon every occasion, yet shows that, in matters of weight and moment, this may sometimes not only be lawful, but duty.

2:11–14 In this Paul finds himself obliged to oppose Peter, for *he was to be blamed*, a plain evidence that he was not inferior to him, and consequently of the pope's pretence to supremacy and infallibility, as the successor of Peter.

3:8 The design was that all who believed on Christ, whether Jews or Gentiles, might become heirs of Abraham's blessing, and particularly of that great promise of the Spirit, which was peculiarly reserved for the times of the gospel.

3:16 '*That seed is Christ*'—So the covenant is still in force; for Christ abideth for ever in his person, and in his spiritual seed, who are his by faith.

3:19 Though the law, considered as the law of nature, is always in force, and still continues to be of use, to convince men of sin, and to restrain them from it, yet we are now no longer under the bondage and terror of that legal covenant.

3:27 Having in baptism professed their faith in him, they were thereby devoted to him. Being baptized into Christ, we are baptized into his death, that as he died and rose again, so, in conformity thereunto, we should die unto sin, and walk in newness of life (Rom. 6:3–4). It would be of great advantage to us did we oftener remember this.

4:11 The labour of ministers is in vain upon those who begin in the Spirit and end in the flesh, who, though they seem to set out well, yet afterwards turn aside from the way of the gospel. Note, those will have a great deal to answer for upon whom the faithful ministers of Jesus Christ bestow labour in vain.

6:14 This is a temper of mind that all Christians should be labouring after; and the best way to attain it is to converse much with the cross of Christ.

Ephesians

1:11 All who are chosen to happiness as the end are chosen to holiness as the means.

1:13–14 The gift of the Holy Ghost, all his influences and operations, both as a sanctifier and a comforter, are heaven begun, glory in the seed and bud.

1:19 It is a difficult thing to bring a soul to believe in Christ, and to venture its all upon his righteousness, and upon the hope of eternal life. It is nothing less than an almighty power that will work this in us.

3:17 Faith opens the door of the soul to receive Christ; faith admits him, and submits to him.

4:11 The great gift that Christ gave to the church at his ascension was that of the ministry of peace and reconciliation. The gift of the ministry is the fruit of Christ's ascension.

4:13 Now we shall never come to the perfect man, till we come to the perfect world.

6:6 A steady regard to the Lord Jesus Christ will make men faithful and sincere in every station of life. Service performed with conscience, and from a regard to God, though it be to unrighteous masters, will be accounted by Christ as service done to himself.

6:11 Here is a Christian in complete armour. It is observable that, among them all, there is none for the back; if we turn our back upon the enemy, we lie exposed.

Philippians

1:6 The confidence of Christians is the great comfort of Christians.

1:12 A strange chemistry of Providence this, to extract so great a good as the enlargement of the gospel out of so great an evil as the confinement of the apostle.

1:23 As soon as the soul departs, it is immediately with Christ.

1:27 There may be a oneness of heart and affection among Christians, where there is diversity of judgment and apprehensions about many things.

2:26–27 But why did not the apostle heal him, who was endued with a power of curing diseases, as well as raising the dead? Probably because that was intended as a sign to others, and to confirm the truth of the gospel, and therefore needed not be exercised one towards another. And perhaps they had not that power at all times, and at their own discretion, but only when some great end was to be served by it, and when God saw fit.

3:9 The Lord Jesus Christ is the Lord our righteousness. Had he not been God, he could not have been our righteousness; the transcendent excellence of the divine nature put such a value upon, and such a virtue into, his sufferings, that they became sufficient to satisfy for the sins of the world, and to bring in a righteousness which will be effectual to all that believe. Faith is the ordained means of actual interest and saving benefit in all the purchase of his blood.

4:4 Joy in God is a duty of great consequence in the Christian life; and Christians need to be again and again called to it.

4:6 Avoid anxious care and distracting thought in the wants and difficulties of life. Observe, it is the duty and interest of Christians to live without care. There is a care of diligence, which is our duty, and consists in a wise forecast and due concern; but there is a care of diffidence and distrust which is our sin and folly, and which only perplexes and distracts the mind.

4:7 This peace ... will keep us from sinning under our troubles, and from sinking under them.

Colossians

1:2 Faithfulness runs through every character and relation of the Christian life, and is the crown and glory of them all.

1:11 He prays not only that they may be *supported* under their troubles, but *strengthened* for them; the reason is there is work to be done even when we are suffering.

1:27 The ground of our hope is Christ in the word, or the gospel revelation, declaring the nature and methods of obtaining it. The evidence of our hope is Christ in the heart, or the sanctification of the soul, and its preparation for the heavenly glory.

3:3 Our true life lies in the other world ... at the second coming of Christ we hope for the perfection of our happiness. Our head is there, our home is there, our treasure is there, and we hope to be there for ever.

3:5 Covetousness is spiritual idolatry: it is the giving of that love and regard to worldly wealth which are due to God only, and carries a greater degree of malignity in it, and is more highly provoking to God, than is commonly thought.

4:14 Skill in physic is a useful accomplishment in a minister and may be improved to more extensive usefulness and greater esteem among Christians.

1 Thessalonians

1:10 There is good reason to hope and wait for his coming, because he has delivered us from the wrath to come.

2:19 It is in heaven that holy souls shall meet, and never part more.

4:1 It is not enough that we abide in the faith of the gospel, but we must abound in the work of faith. We must not only persevere to the end, but we should grow better, and walk more evenly and closely with God.

4:14 His resurrection is a full confirmation of all that is said in the gospel, or by the word of the Lord, which has *brought life and immortality to life*.

4:16 He will descend from heaven into this our air.

4:17 Those who did not sleep in death will have no greater privilege or joy at that day than those who fell asleep in Jesus. Those that shall be found alive will then be changed. At, or immediately before, this rapture into the clouds, those who are alive will undergo a mighty change, which will be equivalent to dying.

5:5 The Lord will come to them as a friend in the day, not as a thief in the night.

5:12 They are called labourers, and should not be loiterers.

5:20 By *prophesyings* here we are to understand the preaching of the word, the interpreting and applying of the scriptures.

5:24 The faithfulness of God was their security that they should persevere to the end.

5:25 The more people pray for their ministers the more good ministers may have from God, and the more benefit people may receive by their ministry.

2 Thessalonians

1:9 They shall be always dying, and yet never die. It must needs be so, since the punishment is inflicted by an eternal God, fastening upon an immortal soul, set out of the reach of divine mercy and grace.

3:1 Those who are at a great distance may meet together at the throne of grace.

1 Timothy

1:13 Unbelief is at the bottom of what sinners do ignorantly; they do not believe God's threatenings, otherwise they could not do as they do.

1:17 When we have found God good we must not forget to pronounce him great; and his kind thoughts of us must not at all abate our high thoughts of him, but rather increase them.

2:2 The summit of the ambition of a good Christian is to lead a quiet and peaceable life, to get through the world unmolested in a low private station.

2:4 This one God *will have all men to be saved* … not that he has decreed the salvation of all, for then all men would be saved; but he has a good will to the salvation of all, and none perish but by their own fault (Matt. 23:37).

God has a good will to the salvation of all; so that it is not so much the want of a will in God to save them as it is a want of will in them to be saved in God's way.

2:5 It is observable that the unity of God is asserted and joined with the unity of the Mediator; and the church of Rome might as well maintain a plurality of gods as a plurality of mediators.

2:6 The mediation of Christ extends itself thus far to all the children of men that he paid a price sufficient for the salvation of all mankind.

3:6 Take heed of pride, because it is a sin that turned angels into devils.

5:17 The presbytery ruled, and the same that ruled were those *who laboured in the word and doctrine*: they had not one to preach to them and another to rule them.

6:12 Those who will get to heaven must fight their way thither.

6:17 Ministers must not be afraid of the rich; be they ever so rich, they must speak to them, and charge them.

2 Timothy

1:5 It is a comfortable thing when children imitate the faith and holiness of their godly parents, and tread in their steps.

2:8 The incarnation and resurrection of Jesus Christ, heartily believed and rightly considered, will support a Christian under all sufferings in the present life.

2:22 Youthful lusts are very dangerous, for which reason even hopeful young people should be warned of them, for they war against the soul (1 Peter 2:11).

3:16–17 The same Spirit that breathed reason into us breathes revelation among us. O that we may love our Bibles more, and keep closer to them than ever!

4:13 Whereas he had exhorted Timothy to give attendance to reading, so he did himself, though he was now ready to be offered. As long as we live, we must still be learning.

Titus

2:13 His first coming was in meanness, to satisfy justice and purchase happiness; his second will be in majesty, to bestow and instate his people in it.

Christ then is the *great God*, not figuratively, as magistrates and others are sometimes called gods, or as appearing and acting in the name of God, but properly and absolutely, *the true God*.

3:5 Election is of grace: we are chosen *to be* holy, not because it was antecedently seen that we should be so (Eph. 1:4). It is the fruit, not the cause of election.

We must be initially saved now, by regeneration, if on good ground we would expect complete salvation in heaven. The change then will be but in degree, not in kind. Grace is glory begun, as glory is but grace in its perfection.

Philemon

1:1 A lover of good men is one property of a good minister (Titus 1:8), and especially must such love those who labour with them in the work of the gospel, and who are faithful therein.

1:3 *Grace*, the free favour and good-will of God, the spring and fountain of all blessings; *and peace*, all good, as the fruit and effect of that grace.

1:4–6 Our prayers and praises should be offered up to God, not for ourselves only, but for others also.

1:17 Wise and good ministers will have great and tender care of young converts, to encourage and hearten them what they can to and in their duty.

1:19 How great the endearments are between ministers and those towards whom their endeavours have been blessed to their conversion or spiritual edification!

1:20 Philemon was Paul's son in the faith, yet he entreats him as a brother; Onesimus a poor slave, yet he solicits for him as if he were seeking some great thing for himself.

1:21 Good persons will be ready for good works, and not narrow and pinching, but abundant in them (Isa. 32:8).

1:22 Prayer of people for ministers, especially when they are in distress and danger, is their great duty; ministers need and request it. Paul, though an apostle, did so with much earnestness (Rom. 15:30).

1:25 This Lord Jesus Christ is *ours* by original title to us, and by gospel offers and gift, his purchase of us, and our own acceptance of him, resignation to him, and mystical union with him: *Our Lord Jesus Christ*.

Hebrews

1:1 Now we must expect no new revelation, but only more of the Spirit of Christ to help us better to understand what is already revealed.

1:4 The superior nature of Christ is proved from his superior name. The superiority of the name and nature of Christ above the angels is declared in the holy scriptures, and to be deduced thence.

1:11–12 Sin has made a great change in the world for the worse, and Christ will make a great change in it for the better. Christ lives to take care of us while we live, and of ours when we are gone, and this should quicken us all to make our interest in him clear and sure, that our spiritual and eternal life may be hid with Christ in God.

1:14 Angels ... are spirits without bodies or inclination to bodies, and yet they can assume bodies, and appear in them, when God pleases.

2:5 Christ has the administration of the gospel church, which at once bespeaks Christ's honour and the church's happiness and safety.

2:10 He was made perfect through sufferings; that is, he perfected the work of our redemption by shedding his blood, and was thereby perfectly qualified to be a Mediator between God and man.

2:11 God is the Father of Christ by eternal generation and by miraculous conception, of Christians by adoption and regeneration.

2:13 Christ's children were given him of the Father, in the counsel of his eternal love, and that covenant of peace which was between them. And they are given to Christ at their conversion. When they take hold of his covenant, then Christ receives them, rules over them, rejoices in them, perfects all their affairs, takes them up to heaven, and there presents them to his Father, *Behold, I and the children which thou hast given me.*

2:14 Death is not only a conquered enemy, but a reconciled friend, not sent to hurt the soul, or separate it from the love of God, but to put an end to all their grievances and complaints, and to give them a passage to eternal life and blessedness; so that to them death is not now in the hand of Satan, but in the hand of Christ—not Satan's servant—has not hell following it, but heaven to all who are in Christ.

4:16 We should every day put up a petition for mercy in our last day.

6:1 As those who are grown Christians must be willing to hear the plainest truths preached for the sake of the weak, so the weak must be willing to hear the more difficult and mysterious truths preached for the sake of those who are strong.

6:13 God never needs to change his counsels; for nothing new can arise to him who sees the end from the beginning.

6:19 An unseen Jesus within the veil is the foundation of his hope; the free grace of God, the merits and mediation of Christ, and the powerful influences of his Spirit, are the grounds of his hope, and so it is a steadfast hope.

9:27 This is matter of comfort to the godly, that they shall die well and die but once; but it is matter of terror to the wicked, who die in their sins, that they cannot return again to do that great work better.

9:28 It is the distinguishing character of true believers that they are looking for Christ; they look to him by faith; they look for him by hope and holy desires.

10:25 There is a trying day coming on us all, the day of our death, and we should observe all the signs of it approaching, and improve them to greater watchfulness and diligence in duty.

11:3 By faith we understand much more of the formation of the world than ever could be understood by the naked eye of natural reason. The Bible gives us the truest and most exact account of the origin of all things, and we are to believe it, and not to wrest or run down the scripture-account of the creation, because it does not suit with some fantastic hypotheses of our own, which has been in some learned but conceited men the first remarkable step towards infidelity, and has led them into many more.

11:25 Suffering is to be chosen rather than sin, there being more evil in the least sin than there can be in the greatest suffering.

12:2–3 Compare Christ's sufferings and ours; and we shall find that as his sufferings far exceeded ours, in the nature and measure of them, so his patience far excels ours, and is a perfect pattern for us to imitate.

12:25 The canon of scripture is now perfected, *the Spirit of prophecy has ceased*, the mystery of God is finished, he has put his last hand to it.

13:5 *God hath said, I will never leave thee, nor forsake thee.* This was said to Joshua (Josh. 1:5) but belongs to all the faithful servants of God.

13:10 The Lord's table is not our altar, but it is furnished with provision from the altar. The Lord's supper is the feast of the gospel Passover.

James

1:2 Philosophy may instruct men to be calm under their troubles; but Christianity teaches them to be joyful, because such exercises proceed from love and not fury in God.

1:5 Let us confess our want of wisdom to God and daily ask it of him.

1:20 The worst thing we can bring to a religious controversy is anger.

2:14–26 When Paul says that *a man is justified by faith, without the deeds of the law* (Rom. 3:28), he plainly speaks of another sort of work than James does, but not of another sort of faith. Paul speaks of works wrought in obedience to the law of Moses, and before men's embracing the faith of the gospel; but James speaks of works done in obedience to the gospel, and as the proper and necessary effects and fruits of sound believing in Christ Jesus.

The justification of which Paul speaks is different from that spoken of by James; the one speaks of our persons being justified before God, the other speaks of our faith being justified before men.

2:25 To rehearse that article of our creed, therefore, *I believe in God the Father Almighty*, will not distinguish us from devils at last, unless we now give up ourselves to God as the gospel directs, and love him, and delight ourselves in him, and serve him, which the devils do not, cannot do.

3:1 These words do not forbid doing what we can to direct and instruct others in the way of their duty or to reprove them in a Christian way for what is amiss; but we must not affect to speak and act as those who are continually assuming the chair, we must not prescribe to one another, so as to make our own sentiments a standard by which to try all others, because God gives various gifts to men, and expects from each according to that measure of light which he gives.

4:7 Resolution shuts and bolts the door against temptation.

4:8 Those that draw nigh to God in a way of duty shall find God drawing nigh to them in a way of mercy.

4:10 The highest honour in heaven will be the reward of the greatest humility on earth.

5:11 The best way to bear afflictions is to look to the end of them. The tender mercy of God is such that he will make his people an abundant amends for all their sufferings and afflictions. Let us serve our God, and endure our trials, as those who believe the end will crown all.

5:13 In the original it is only said *sing*, without the addition of psalms or any other word. We learn from Pliny, Justin Martyr and Tertullian, that the Christians were accustomed to sing hymns, either taken out of scripture, or of more private composure, in their worship of God.

5:14–15 In Mark's gospel we read of the apostle anointing many that were sick and healing them (Mark 6:13). And we have accounts of this being practised in the church two hundred years after Christ; but then the gift of healing also accompanied it, and, when the miraculous gift ceased, this rite was laid aside.

1 Peter

1:7 God's design in afflicting his people is their probation, not their destruction; their advantage, not their ruin: a *trial*, as the word signifies, is an experiment or search made upon a man, by some affliction, to prove the value and strength of his faith.

1:13 A Christian's work is not over as soon as he has got into a state of grace; he must still hope and strive for more grace. When he has entered the strait gate, he must still walk in the narrow way, and gird up the loins of his mind for that purpose.

1:21 The resurrection of Christ, considered as an act of power, is common to all the three persons, but as an act of judgment it is peculiar to the Father, who as a Judge released Christ, raised him from the grave, and gave him glory, proclaimed him to all the world to be his Son by his resurrection from the dead, advanced him to heaven, crowned him with glory and honour, invested him with all power in heaven and earth, and glorified him with that glory which he had with God before the world was.

3:1–6 Where the hypocrite's work ends, there the true Christian's work begins.

3:19 Notice the hearers. Because they were dead and disembodied when the apostle speaks of them, therefore he properly calls them spirits now *in prison*; not that they were *in prison when Christ preached to them*, as the vulgar Latin translation and the popish expositors pretend.

5:2 Pastors must be *examples to the flock*, and practise the holiness, self-denial, mortification, and all other Christian duties, which they preach and recommend to their people … regarding the flock more than the fleece.

2 Peter

1:1 True saving faith is a precious grace, and that not only as it is very uncommon, very scarce, even in the visible church, a very small number of true believers among a great multitude of visible professors (Matt. 22:14), but true faith is very excellent and of very great use and advantage to those who have it.

1:21 The very words of scripture are to be accounted the words of the Holy Ghost, and all the plainness and simplicity, all the power and virtue, all the elegance and propriety, of the very words and expressions are to be regarded by us as proceeding from God.

2:1 They reject … the only Saviour and Redeemer of men, who paid a price sufficient to redeem as many worlds of sinners as there are sinners in the world.

2:3 There is no place nor state between the height of glory and the depth of misery in which they shall be allowed to rest. The last degree of torment is not till the day of judgment. The sinning angels, though in hell already, are yet reserved to the judgment of the great day.

3:5 It is hard to persuade men to believe what they are not willing to find true; they are ignorant, in many cases, because they are willing to be ignorant, and they do not know because they do not care to know.

3:7 Give diligence therefore to be found in Christ, that that may be a time of refreshment and day of redemption to you which will be a day of indignation and wrath to the ungodly world.

3:11 All our conversation, whether with high or low, rich or poor, good or bad, friends or enemies, must be holy.

1 John

1:8 The Christian life is a life of continued repentance, humiliation for and mortification of sin, of continual faith in, thankfulness for and love to the Redeemer, and hopeful joyful expectation of a day of glorious redemption, in which the believer shall be fully and finally acquitted, and sin abolished for ever.

2:18 It is a mysterious portion of providence that antichrists should be permitted; but, when they have come, it is good and safe that disciples should be informed of them; ministers should be *watchmen to the house of Israel.*

2:19 The apostolic doctrine did not convert all whom it convinced of its truth.

3:1 Let the followers of Christ be content with hard fare here, since they are in a land of strangers, among those who little know them, and their Lord was so treated before them.

5:16 We cannot pray that the sins of the impenitent and unbelieving should, while they are such, be forgiven them, or that any mercy of life or soul, that supposes the forgiveness of sin, should be granted to them, while they continue such. But we may pray for their repentance, for their being enriched with faith in Christ, and thereupon for all other saving mercies.

2 John

1:2 We should not be religious merely by fits and starts, in certain moods and moons; but religion should still dwell within us, in our minds and hearts, in our faith and love.

1:4 It is joyful to good old ministers, and accordingly to other good old disciples, to see a hopeful rising generation, who may serve God and support religion in the world when they are dead and gone.

1:8 The way to attain the full reward is to abide true to Christ, and constant in religion to the end.

3 John

1:1 To love our friends for the truth's sake is true love, religious gospel love.

1:8 In many ways may the truth be befriended and assisted; those who cannot themselves proclaim it may yet receive, accompany, help and countenance those who do.

Jude

1:1 The apostles were servants before they were apostles, and they were but servants still.

Sanctification is usually spoken of in scripture as the work of the Holy Spirit, yet here it is ascribed to God the Father, because the Spirit works it as the Spirit of the Father and the Son. All who are effectually called are sanctified, *made partakers of a divine nature* (2 Peter 1:4); *for without holiness no man shall see the Lord* (Heb. 12:14).

The called and sanctified are *preserved in Christ Jesus*. As it is God who begins the work of grace in the souls of men, so it is he who carries it on, and perfects it: *He will not forsake the work of his own hands* (Ps. 138:8).

1:3 Those who preach or write of the common salvation should give all diligence to do it well: they should not allow themselves to offer to God or his people that which costs them nothing, or next to nothing, little or no pains or thought (2 Sam. 24:24).

1:5–7 Why may we not content ourselves with staying at home and reading our Bibles? Preaching is not designed to teach us something new in every sermon, somewhat that we knew nothing of before; but *to put us in remembrance*, to call to mind things forgotten, to affect our passions, and engage and fix our resolutions, that our lives may be answerable to our faith.

1:8 Such evil speakers despise the dominion of conscience, make a jest of it, and would banish it out of the world; and as for the word of God, the rule of conscience, they despise it.

1:12 How happy would our world be if men either knew more or practically knew how little they know!

1:14 Christ's coming to judgment was prophesied of as early as the middle of the patriarchal age, and was therefore even then a received and acknowledged truth.

1:15 'Godly' or 'ungodly' signifies little with men now-a-days, unless it be to scoff at and deride even the very expressions; but it is not so in the language of the Holy Ghost.

1:24 When believers shall be presented faultless it will be with exceeding joy. Alas! Now our faults fill us with fears, doubts and sorrows. But *be of good cheer* ... we shall be *presented faultless*; where there is no sin there will be no sorrow, where there is the perfection of holiness, there will be the perfection of joy.

Revelation

1:10 Those who would enjoy communion with God on the Lord's day must endeavour to abstract their thoughts and affections from flesh and fleshly things, and be wholly taken up with things of a spiritual nature.

2:1 It is the honour of God that he knows the number of the stars, calls them by their names, *binds the sweet influences of Pleiades and looses the bands of Orion*; and it is the honour of the Lord Jesus Christ that the ministers of the gospel, who are greater blessings to the church than the stars are to the world, are in his hand. He directs all their motions; he disposes of them into their several orbs; he fills them with light and influence; he supports them, or else they would soon be falling stars; they are instruments in his hand, and all the good they do is by his hand with them.

2:8 His death we commemorate every sacrament day; his resurrection and life every sabbath day.

2:12 It is a *sword with two edges*; it turns and cuts every way. There is the *edge* of the law against the transgressors of that dispensation, and the *edge* of the gospel against the despisers of that dispensation; there is an edge to make a wound, and an edge to open a festered wound in order to its healing.

3:5 Those who walk with Christ in the clean garments of real practical holiness here, and keep themselves unspotted from the world, shall walk with Christ in the white robes of honour and glory in the other world: this is a suitable reward.

3:8 Obedience, fidelity and a free confession of the name of Christ are the fruits of true grace, and are pleasing to Christ as such.

3:10 The same divine grace that has made them fruitful in times of peace will make them faithful in times of persecution.

4:1 We can know nothing of future events but what God is pleased to discover to us; they are within the veil, till God opens the door.

4:3 The rainbow looked like *the emerald*; the most prevailing colour was a pleasant green, to show the reviving and refreshing nature of the new covenant.

6:2 When Christ was going to war, one would think a helmet had been more proper than a crown; but a crown was given him as the earnest and emblem of victory.

6:6 When a people loathe their spiritual food, God may justly deprive them of their daily bread.

6:11 There is a number of Christians, known to God, who are appointed as *sheep for the slaughter*, set apart to be God's witnesses.

7:9 God will have a greater harvest of souls among the Gentiles than he had among the Jews: *More are the children of the desolate than of the married woman.*

7:14 It is not the blood of the martyrs themselves, but the blood of the Lamb, that can wash away sin, and make the soul pure and clean in the sight of God. Other blood stains; this is the only blood that makes the robes of the saints white and clean.

8:3 All the saints are a praying people; none of the children of God are born dumb, a Spirit of grace is always a Spirit of adoption and supplication, teaching us to cry, *Abba, Father.*

8:7 The most severe calamities have their bounds and limits set them by the great God.

8:12 God gives warning to men of his judgments before he sends them; he sounds an alarm by the written word, by ministers, by men's own consciences, and by the signs of the times; so that if a people be surprised, it is their own fault.

9:7–8 They had all the allurements of seeming beauty, to ensnare and defile the minds of men—*hair like women*; their way of worship was very gaudy and ornamental.

9:17 It is Mr Mede's opinion that this is a prediction of great guns, those instruments of cruelty which make such destruction ... these were first used by the Turks at the siege of Constantinople, and, being new and strange, were very terrible, and did great execution.

He who is the Lord of hosts has vast armies at his command, to serve his own purposes—the most formidable powers have limits set them, which they cannot transgress.

12:10 Let us therefore take heed that we give him no cause of accusation against us; and that, when we have sinned, we presently go in before the Lord, and accuse and condemn ourselves, and commit our cause to Christ as our Advocate.

13:18 The most admired dissertation on this intricate subject is that of Dr Potter, where the curious may find sufficient entertainment.

14:1 A counterfeit lamb is mentioned as rising out of the earth in the last chapter, which was really a dragon; here Christ appears as the true paschal Lamb, to show that his mediatorial government is the fruit of his sufferings, and the cause of his people's safety and fidelity.

18:5 When the sins of a people reach up to heaven, the wrath of God will reach down to the earth.

19:1–3 The surest way to have our deliverances continued and completed is to give God the glory for what he has done for us. Praising God for what we have is praying in the most effectual manner for what is yet further to be done for us; the praises of the saints blow up the fire of God's wrath against the common enemy.

20:6 We know something of what the first death is, and it is awful; but we know not what this second death is. It must be much more dreadful; it is the death of the soul, eternal separation from God.

20:12 Happy are those who have so ordered and stated their cause according to the gospel as to know beforehand that they shall be justified in the great day of the Lord.

21:10 Those who would have clear views of heaven must get as near heaven as they can, into the mount of vision, the mount of meditation and faith, whence, as from the top of Pisgah, they may behold the goodly land of the heavenly Canaan.

22:21 Nothing should be more desired by us than that the grace of Christ may be with us in this world, to prepare us for the glory of Christ in the other world.

Appendix. A selection of authors Matthew Henry quoted[1]

Bacon, Lord Francis, 1st Viscount St Alban (1561–1626), philosopher, statesman, lawyer and father of the scientific method

Baxter, Richard, (1615–1691), Puritan gospel preacher at Kidderminster and author of *The Saints' Everlasting Rest* (1650)

Blackmore, Sir Richard, (1654–1729), physician and writer

Bochart, Samuel, (1599–1667), French Protestant

Calvin, John, (1509–1564), French-born Reformer, founder of a theocracy in Geneva, and author of *Institutes of the Christian Religion* and commentaries on most books of the Bible

Calvisius, Sethus, (1556 –1615), German music theorist, composer, chronologer, astronomer and teacher of the late Renaissance

Cave, Dr William, (1637–1713), English divine who successively held the livings of Islington (1662), All-Hallows the Great, Thames Street, London (1679), and Isleworth, Middlesex (1690); chaplain to Charles II

Chrysostom, John, (c. 349–407), Archbishop of Constantinople and an important Early Church Father

Clarke, Dr Samuel, (1675–1729), English philosopher and Anglican clergyman

Cumberland, Richard, (1632–1718), Bishop of Peterborough

Cyprian, Saint, (died a martyr, 14 September 258), Bishop of Carthage and an important early Christian writer

Dod, John, (1550–1645), clergyman and Puritan leader; ordained at Ely in 1580 and ejected in 1607; known as 'Decalogue Dod' after his publication with Robert Cleaver of *A Plaine and Familiar Exposition of the Ten Commandments*, a copy of which was possessed by John Bunyan

Epiphanius of Salamis (c. 310–403), Bishop of Salamis and Metropolitan of Cyprus at the end of the 4th century, and an Early Church Father

Eusebius (c. 263–339), Bishop of Caesarea in Palestine from around 314

Foxe, John, (1517–1587), English historian and martyrologist, the author of *Foxe's Book of Martyrs*

Fuller, Dr Francis, (1636?–1701), curate of Winkworth, Northamptonshire, from which he was ejected; later assistant at Crutched Friars, Mark Lane, London

Goodwin, Dr Thomas, (1600–1680), English Puritan theologian and preacher, and an important leader of religious Independents; served as chaplain to Oliver Cromwell

Gregory, John, (1607–1646), orientalist noted for his biblical scholarship

Grotius, Hugo, (1583–1645), Dutch jurist, theologian, playwright and poet

Hall, Joseph, (1574–1656), Bishop of Exeter (1627) then Norwich (1632)

Hammond, Dr Henry, (1605–1660), English royalist cleric who wrote *Paraphrase and Annotations on the New Testament* and an incomplete work of a similar nature on the Old Testament

Herbert, George, (1593–1633), metaphysical poet and Rector of Bemerton

Hierom (Jerome), Saint, (c. 347–420), ordained priest in Antioch; later secretary to Pope Damasus in Rome; wrote the Vulgate, the first translation of the Hebrew Bible into Latin

Hooper, John, (c. 1495–1555), English churchman and Anglican Bishop of Gloucester and Worcester; martyred during the Marian Persecutions as a Protestant Reformer

Josephus (37–c. 100), Jewish historian who became a Roman citizen

Lightfoot, Dr John, (1602–1675), Hebraist and biblical scholar, Rector of Much Munden and member of the Westminster Assembly of Divines

Martyr, Justin (Flavius Iustinus), (103–165), born at Shechem (Nablus) and martyred in Rome

Masius, Andreas, (1516–1573), born near Brussels; orientalist, lawyer, and counsellor to the Duke of Cleves

Mede, Joseph, (1586–1638), Fellow of Christ's College, Cambridge, theologian and millenarian

Origen (c. 185–254), an early Christian African scholar and theologian

Patrick, Simon, (1626–1707), Bishop of Ely

Perkins, William, (1558–1602), Rector of St Andrew's, Cambridge, and a theologian; one of the foremost leaders of the Puritan movement in the Church of England

Pierson (probably Pearson), John, (1612–1686), Bishop of Chester, theologian and scholar, praised by Richard Baxter

Plutarch (46–120), Greek biographer and essayist

Poole, Matthew, (1624?–1679), biblical commentator and rector of St Michael-le-Querne

Potter, Dr Francis, (1594–1678), clergyman (Rector of Kilmington), inventor, and author of *An Interpretation of the Number 666* (1642)

Raleigh, Sir Walter, (c. 1554–1618), explorer, volunteer for the Huguenot cause in France, and a favourite of Queen Elizabeth I

Sanchuniathon of Beirut (700 BC or earlier), quoted by Eusebius

Seneca (c. 1 BC–AD 65), Roman Stoic philosopher

Spencer, Dr John, (1630–1693), Dean of Ely

Tallents, Francis, (1619–1708), clergyman and ejected minister

Tertullian (c. 160–c. 220), prolific early Christian author from Carthage in the Roman province of Africa; the oldest extant Latin writer to use the term 'Trinity' and to give a formal exposition of Trinitarian theology

Tillotson, John, (1630–1694), Archbishop of Canterbury

Vermigli, Peter Martyr, (1499–1562), former prior of a convent in Naples who adopted Reformed beliefs; influential in modifying the *Book of Common Prayer*

Whiston, William, (1667–1752), natural philosopher and theologian

Whitby, Dr Daniel, DD (1638–1726), Rector of St Edmund, Salisbury

Notes

1 Information gleaned from Wikipedia (accessed 2012); *The Oxford Dictionary of National Biography* (Oxford: Oxford University Press; online edn. at www.oxforddnb.com, 2004–2012); and **Una McGovern, (ed.),** *Chambers Biographical Dictionary* (Edinburgh: Chambers Harrap, 2005).

About Day One:

Day One's threefold commitment:

- To be faithful to the Bible, God's inerrant, infallible Word;
- To be relevant to our modern generation;
- To be excellent in our publication standards.

I continue to be thankful for the publications of Day One. They are biblical; they have sound theology; and they are relative to the issues at hand. The material is condensed and manageable while, at the same time, being complete—a challenging balance to find. We are happy in our ministry to make use of these excellent publications.

JOHN MACARTHUR, PASTOR-TEACHER, GRACE COMMUNITY CHURCH, CALIFORNIA

It is a great encouragement to see Day One making such excellent progress. Their publications are always biblical, accessible and attractively produced, with no compromise on quality. Long may their progress continue and increase!

JOHN BLANCHARD, AUTHOR, EVANGELIST AND APOLOGIST

Visit our website for more information and to request a free catalogue of our books.

www.dayone.co.uk

The Gospel in Genesis
From Fig Leaves to Faith

D MARTYN LLOYD-JONES

144PP PAPERBACK, ISBN 978–1–84625–137–5

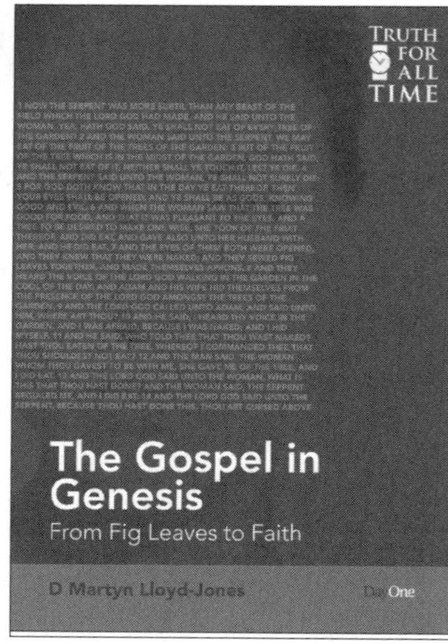

If you've ever asked, 'Why am I the way that I am? Why is life so hard? Is there any hope?' you'll find answers in Martyn Lloyd-Jones's study of Genesis.

In this series of never-before-published sermons, beloved teacher Martyn Lloyd-Jones walks readers through the early chapters of Genesis. *The Gospel in Genesis* starts with the fall of man and ends with the call of Abram as it examines portions of chapters 3–12. Along the way, Lloyd-Jones talks of serpents and sin, of the Word of God and the Babel of man. But the destination of *The Gospel in Genesis* is clear: readers will be moved from fig leaves in the garden to faith in the gospel.

Thus Lloyd-Jones preaches the gospel of Jesus Christ from the pages of Genesis. These nine sermons will snap nonbelievers out of their apathy toward God and will embolden believers to share the only gospel that offers answers to life's biggest questions.

Dr D Martyn Lloyd-Jones (1899–1981) was minister of Westminster Chapel in London for thirty years. His many books have brought profound spiritual encouragement to millions around the world. He believed that, even in a secular age, people respond to the uncompromising truth—a view which was confirmed as he saw the liberal churches emptying and the evangelicals maintaining their cause.

The Sovereignty and Supremacy of King Jesus
Bowing to the Gracious Despot

MIKE ABENDROTH

240PP PAPERBACK, ISBN 978–1–84625–267–9

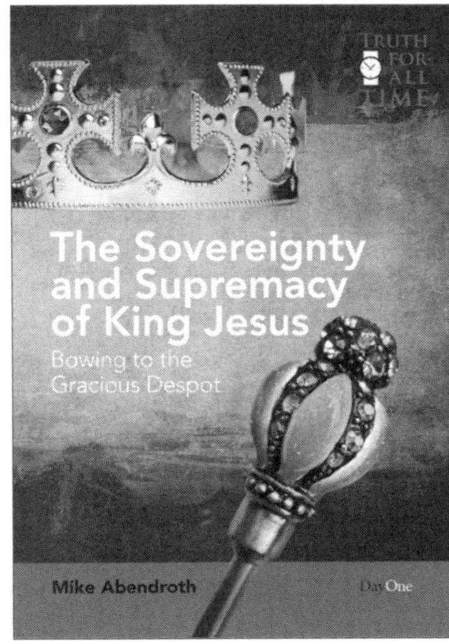

What thoughts flood our minds when we think about God? Do we think of Him as King? If so, what kind of King? In this book Mike Abendroth seeks to address a twofold problem: most Christians do not consider God as any type of Monarch, and, if they do, they think about monarchs that are weak rather than reflecting on the utter Lordship of God, the ultimate King.

In Part 1, Mike Abendroth demonstrates that the whole Bible reveals God as King. In Part 2, he describes the life-changing implications that flow from that revelation. Filled with insightful quotations, worshipful hymns, and thoughtful study questions, this book helps us to biblically embrace God as our King.

Mike Abendroth graduated from The Master's Seminary (M. Div.) in 1996 and became the pastor of Bethlehem Bible Church, West Boylston, MA, in 1997. He received his Doctorate of Ministry in Expository Preaching at the Southern Baptist Theological Seminary in 2006. One of his passions is training men to teach the Bible expositionally. He is the author of *Jesus Christ: the Prince of Preachers* (Day One, 2008). Mike is married to Kimberly and they have four children.

I wholeheartedly endorse this book and strongly encourage you to carefully read its message. Mark up its pages. Devour its truths. Share it with others. Use it as an evangelistic tool. Draw from it to preach. Use it to teach small group Bible studies. You will find this book to be an invaluable resource.
STEVEN J. LAWSON, SENIOR PASTOR, CHRIST FELLOWSHIP BAPTIST CHURCH, MOBILE, ALABAMA

I Believe ...
The Apostles' Creed Simply Explained

TIMOTHY CROSS

128PP PAPERBACK, ISBN 978–1–84625–201–3

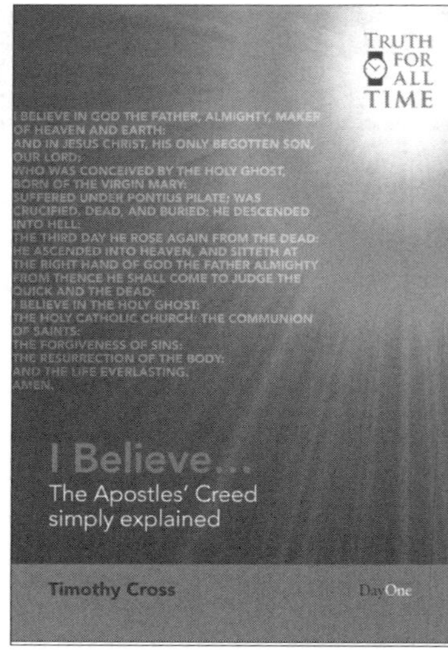

Christians should be well grounded in the faith 'which was once for all delivered to the saints' (Jude 3). We should know what we believe, why we believe it, and the scriptural basis for our beliefs. In this book, Timothy Cross provides a 'primer' in the key doctrines of Christianity as he explains each line of the Apostles' Creed, one of the clearest and most succinct distillations of the Christian faith ever written. Whether you are a Christian of many years' standing, a new Christian, or just interested in the Christian faith, read this book to gain a firmer grounding in the fundamentals of biblical Christianity.

Timothy Cross comes from Cardiff, Wales, and has lived in Belfast, Northern Ireland. He studied Theology at Cardiff University and then trained as an RE and Games teacher at Aberystwyth University. He is the author of over twenty Christian books and numerous articles in Christian periodicals. In 2002 he was awarded an honorary Doctor of Sacred Literature by the Christian Bible College, Rocky Mount, North Carolina, in recognition of his written ministry. Dr Cross has a preaching/Bible teaching ministry and since 1989 has broadcast a monthly Bible-based message on the South Wales Talking Magazine. His life's passions include biblical languages, distance running and the beaches of South Wales.

Timothy Cross has a passion for making truth both interesting and infectious. This exploration of the Apostles' Creed is an example of his love for the Bible and his desire to make it relevant to today's generation. I thoroughly recommend this volume.
—Dr Derek W. H. Thomas, Professor of Theology, Reformed Theological Seminary, Jackson, USA

Taste and See That the Lord is Good

JOEL JAMES

208PP PAPERBACK, ISBN 978–1–84625–269–3

How do you relate to God? Moses said to Israel, 'You shall fear the LORD your God; you shall serve Him and cling to Him …' (Deut. 10:20). In other words, knowing God is a perfect paradox: He is both too great to approach and too great not to. When we study the God of the Bible, we should be both overwhelmed by His incomparable majesty and irresistibly drawn to His love.

In this warm and easy-to-read study of the attributes of God, Joel James captures and encourages that worshipful blend of awestruck fear and irrepressible love. Because it is built around key Old Testament 'Sunday school' stories of God's working with people such as Moses, Jonah, Ahab, and Manasseh, this book avoids the pitfalls of philosophical abstraction. It won't simply teach you who God is, it will also help you to love Him.

Joel James has an M.Div. and a D.Min. from The Master's Seminary and is the pastor-teacher of Grace Fellowship in Pretoria, South Africa. He and his wife, Ruth, have been married since 1993 and have two children.

In *Taste and See That the Lord Is Good,* Joel James has produced an intensely practical tool for the church at large. The result of his fresh angle and dynamic style is an easily comprehended introduction to the person of God. Because of the thorough expositions contained in this book, the resulting portrait of God is as deep as it is vibrant, serving as an accessible resource to anyone seeking to better understand the nature and character of God.

Dr John MacArthur, Pastor-Teacher, Grace Community Church, Sun Valley, California